Recruiting
Employees

FOUNDATIONS FOR ORGANIZATIONAL SCIENCE
A Sage Publications Series

Series Editor

David Whetten, *Brigham Young University*

Editors

Peter J. Frost, *University of British Columbia*
Anne S. Huff, *University of Colorado and Cranfield University (UK)*
Benjamin Schneider, *University of Maryland*
M. Susan Taylor, *University of Maryland*
Andrew Van de Ven, *University of Minnesota*

The FOUNDATIONS FOR ORGANIZATIONAL SCIENCE series supports the development of students, faculty, and prospective organizational science professionals through the publication of texts authored by leading organizational scientists. Each volume provides a highly personal, hands-on introduction to a core topic or theory and challenges the reader to explore promising avenues for future theory development and empirical application.

Books in This Series

Alison E. Barber

Recruiting Employees

Individual and Organizational Perspectives

Foundations for
Organizational
Science
A Sage Publications Series

SAGE Publications
International Educational and Professional Publisher
Thousand Oaks   London   New Delhi

For information:

SAGE Publications, Inc.
2455 Teller Road
Thousand Oaks, California 91320
E-mail: order@sagepub.com

SAGE Publications Ltd.
6 Bonhill Street
London EC2A 4PU
United Kingdom

SAGE Publications India Pvt. Ltd.
M-32 Market
Greater Kailash I
New Delhi 110 048 India

Printed in the United States of America

Library of Congress Cataloging-in-Publication Data

Barber, Alison E.

      Recuiting employees: individual and organizational perspectives /
by Allison E. Barber.
         p.   cm. -- (Foundations of organizational science)
      Includes bibliographical references and index.
      ISBN 0-7619-0942-7 (acid-free paper). -- ISBN 0-7619-0943-5 (pbk.:
acid-free paper)
      1. Employees--Recruiting.   I. Title.   II. Series.
HF5549.5.R44B367 1998
658.3'11--dc21   97-45383

This book is printed on acid-free paper.
98 99 00 01 02 03 04 10 9 8 7 6 5 4 3 2 1

Acquisition Editor:	Marquita Flemming
Editorial Assistant:	Frances Borghi
Production Editor:	Michele Lingre
Editorial Assistant:	Lynn Miyata
Typesetter/Designer:	Rose Tylak
Print Buyer:	Anna Chin

Contents

Acknowledgments

I often tell graduate students that they should enjoy the process of preparing for comprehensive exams, as opportunities to read extensively and contemplate broadly become more and more rare as one's academic responsibilities increase. Writing this book provided me with one of those rare opportunities.

For the most part, the book was written while I was on sabbatical at the University of Maryland. I am grateful to both Michigan State University and the University of Maryland for allowing me to devote much of my year to writing. In addition, I'm grateful to faculty and students in the Department of Management and Organizations at the University of Maryland (Susan Taylor and Cindy Stevens, in particular) for their willingness to serve as sounding boards as I worked on the manuscript. Finally, my thanks to those family members, friends, and colleagues who made my transitions (from Michigan to Maryland, and back again) as easy as they possibly could have been.

I am also grateful to those individuals who read and commented on earlier versions of this manuscript: Jim Breaugh, Sara Rynes, Susan Taylor, Dan Turban, and Michael Wesson. Their comments substantially improved the final version, and their words of encouragement were greatly appreciated. Susan and Mike were especially thorough and thoughtful, and deserve extra thanks for their willingness to reread sections that I revised. I am particularly grateful to Mike for taking time away from his comprehensive exam preparation to read this manuscript. Somehow I don't think he bought the argument that it was a process to be enjoyed.

Introduction to the Series

The title of this series, **Foundations for Organizational Science** (FOS), denotes a distinctive focus. FOS books are educational aids for mastering the core theories, essential tools, and emerging perspectives that constitute the field of organizational science (broadly defined to include organizational behavior, organizational theory, human resource management, and business strategy). The primary objective of this series is to support ongoing professional development among established scholars.

The series was born out of many long conversations among several colleagues, including Peter Frost, Anne Huff, Rick Mowday, Ben Schneider, Susan Taylor, and Andy Van de Ven, over a number of years. From those discussions, we concluded that there has been a major gap in our professional literature, as characterized by the following comment: "If I, or one of my students, want to learn about population ecology, diversification strategies, group dynamics, or personnel selection, we are pretty much limited to academic journal articles or books that are written either for content experts or practitioners. Wouldn't it be wonderful to have access to the teaching notes from a course taught by a master teacher of this topic?"

The plans for compiling a set of learning materials focusing on professional development emerged from our extended discussions of common experiences and observations, including the following:

1. While serving as editors of journals, program organizers for professional association meetings, and mentors for new faculty members, we have observed wide variance in theoretical knowledge and tool proficiency in our field. To the extent that this outcome reflects available learning opportunities, we hope that this series will help "level the playing field."

2. We have all "taught" in doctoral and junior faculty consortia prior to our professional meetings and have been struck by how often the participants comment, "I wish that the rest of the meetings [paper sessions and symposia] were as informative." Such observations got us thinking—Are our doctoral courses more like paper sessions or doctoral consortia? What type of course would constitute a learning experience analogous to attending a doctoral consortium? What materials would we need to teach such a course? We hope that the books in this series have the "touch and feel" of a doctoral consortium workshop.

3. We all have had some exposure to the emerging "virtual university" in which faculty and students in major doctoral programs share their distinctive competencies, either through periodic jointly sponsored seminars or through distance learning technology, and we would like to see these opportunities diffused more broadly. We hope that reading our authors' accounts will be the next best thing to observing them in action.

4. We see some of the master scholars in our field reaching the later stages of their careers, and we would like to "bottle" their experience and insight for future generations. Therefore, this series is an attempt to disseminate "best practices" across space and time.

To address these objectives, we ask authors in this series to pass along their "craft knowledge" to students and faculty beyond the boundaries of their local institutions by writing from the perspective of seasoned teachers and mentors. Specifically, we encourage them to invite readers into their classrooms (to gain an understanding of the past, present, and future of scholarship in particular areas from the perspective of their firsthand experience), as well as into their offices and hallway conversations (to gain insights into the subtleties and nuances of exemplary professional practice).

By explicitly focusing on an introductory doctoral seminar setting, we encourage our authors to address the interests and needs of nonexpert students and colleagues who are looking for answers to questions such as the following: Why is this topic important? How did it originate and how has it evolved? How is it different from related topics? What do we actually know about this topic? How does one effectively communicate this information to students and practitioners? What are the methodological pitfalls and conceptual dead ends that should be avoided? What are the most/least promising opportunities for theory development and empirical study in this area? What questions/situations/phenomena are not well suited for this theory or tool?

What is the most interesting work in progress? What are the most critical gaps in our current understanding that need to be addressed during the next 5 years?

We are pleased to share our dream with you, and we encourage your suggestions for how these books can better satisfy your learning needs—as a newcomer to the field preparing for prelims or developing a research proposal, or as an established scholar seeking to broaden your knowledge and proficiency.

—*DAVID A. WHETTEN*
SERIES EDITOR

1 Introduction

Comments on Scope
What Is Recruitment?
Key Dimensions of Recruitment
    Players
    Activities
    Outcomes
    Context
    Phases
Using the key dimensions to organize and evaluate
    recruitment research
Structure of Remaining Chapters

In recent years, the importance of effective human resource management has been documented both in scholarly research (e.g., Huselid, 1995; MacDuffie, 1995; Welbourne & Andrews, 1996) and in the popular business press (e.g., Fisher, 1997; Ulrich, 1997). It has become increasingly clear that there is a relationship between human resource practices and "bottom line" measures, such as return on assets and investments, profitability, and even organizational survival.

Recruitment is an important part of effective human resource management. Recruitment performs the essential function of drawing an important resource—human capital—into the organization. The success of later human resource efforts, such as selection, training, and compensation, depends in part on the quality and quantity of new employees identified and attracted through the recruitment process. For instance, Boudreau and Rynes (1985) demonstrated that selection utilities can vary dramatically as a function of recruitment practices—in one illustration, by a factor of ten.

Organizations devote considerable resources to recruitment, with average cost-per-hire estimates in the thousands of dollars (Martin & Raju, 1992). Anecdotal reports (e.g., Nakache, 1997; Tully, 1996) further support the importance of recruitment. For example, at Cisco, a successful information technology company that puts a high value on innovative recruitment practices, "the only thing worth more than a bright new idea is a bright new hire" (Nakache, 1997, p. 275).

In addition to its importance to business, recruitment has important consequences for individuals. Recruitment is part of a two-way street: It is the organizational side of a "matching" process that occurs between firms with jobs and individuals seeking jobs. Recruitment is intended to influence applicants' job choices and, because work is a central part of many people's lives, those choices in turn can have a substantial impact on applicants' well-being.

Recruitment's potential significance for both individuals and organizations make it an interesting and relevant topic for research. Indeed, research attention to recruitment issues has risen dramatically over the past 20 years. As one indicator of the emergence of this area, the 1976 version of the Industrial/ Organizational Psychology handbook offered less than a page on recruitment (Guion, 1976), and in the 1991 version an entire 45-page chapter (Rynes, 1991) was devoted to the topic. Yet, although certain aspects of the recruitment process have been studied in great detail, many other important issues have been examined sporadically, if at all. Furthermore, many have argued that existing research in this area is far too simple to adequately capture the complex recruiting environment.

It is not difficult to identify unanswered research questions in this area. What is difficult is choosing, from among the many unanswered questions, those questions whose answers will contribute most to the orderly and systematic accumulation of knowledge about recruitment. The purpose of this book is to compare existing recruitment knowledge to the much broader domain of what we need to know about recruitment and to propose answers to the question, "What should we do next?"

Before we can get to that question, however, we must define the domain of recruitment research. Toward that end, this chapter provides a definition of recruitment and specifies elements relevant to recruitment research. Considered jointly, these elements should provide a clear sense of the complexity of recruitment. They also present a daunting challenge to recruitment researchers wishing to respond to criticisms that their research should be more complex. Therefore, this chapter also offers a strategy for organizing these issues in a way that, I hope, will help clarify future research needs. Subsequent chapters will draw on this strategy as a means of organizing reviews of existing research and identifying promising new directions of research.

Comments on Scope

Four comments about the scope of this book are in order. First, this book focuses on recruitment as distinct from selection. Whereas recruitment is aimed at attracting individuals to an organization, selection is aimed at identifying the most qualified from among those individuals. As Wanous (1980) noted, each of these processes involves "matching" organizations and individuals, but the nature of the matching differs. In selection, applicant abilities are matched with organizational needs, and it is the organization that determines whether a suitable match exists. In recruitment, organizational and job characteristics are matched with individual needs, with the individual assessing the suitability of the match.

This is not to suggest that recruitment and selection are unrelated. In many cases, the recruitment and selection processes occur simultaneously, and it is inevitable that one influences the other (Taylor & Giannantonio, 1993). Very few studies, however, address recruitment and selection jointly. Those that do will be discussed in later chapters, but with an emphasis on what they have to say about recruitment.

Second, though recruitment is an organizational function, it is nonetheless intended to influence individual (job applicant) attitudes and behaviors. Organizational recruitment cannot be understood without considering the individual's perspective. As Schwab (1982) noted, organizational issues and individual issues necessarily go together because the "major outcome— employment—depends on the results of a series of decisions made by both the organization and the individual" (p. 104). Therefore, this book addresses the topic of job choice, and to a lesser extent the broader topic of job search. Again, however, the focus is on how these topics relate to recruitment.

Third, the book focuses exclusively on external recruitment (i.e., recruitment of individuals currently outside the organization) and does not address the many interesting issues raised by internal recruitment (i.e., recruitment of current employees into different positions within the organization). The primary reason for this limitation is that the two types of recruitment entail very different issues (Rynes & Barber, 1990), and combining them into one brief text would necessarily limit the amount of detail that could be offered on either. For example, internal recruitment necessarily involves questions of career planning and development, a topic of substantial research. Furthermore, in practice external and internal recruitment are typically studied as separate processes. Individual scholars focus on one or the other but rarely on both. By limiting discussion to external recruitment, I do not mean to imply that external recruitment is in any way more important or more interesting than internal recruitment, or even that the common practice of studying these issues separately is appropriate. Rather, it is an acknowledgment that the two are most commonly studied separately.

Finally, this book is written for those interested in contributing to the research literature on recruitment. It is not intended as a "how-to" text for those engaged in the practice of recruitment. Nevertheless, recruitment research deals with "real world" problems, and should be judged both on its theoretical value (whether it enhances our understanding of recruitment) and on its practical influence (whether it tells us how to improve recruitment). Both perspectives are addressed in this book; thus, the practitioner who has the patience to wade through the more research-oriented passages should gain a valuable understanding of what we do and do not know about recruitment practices.

What is Recruitment?

Most of us have a "common sense" notion of what recruitment is. Yet providing an explicit definition is useful, if not essential, to researchers, as the development of such definitions can help us identify issues relevant to our research.

Rynes (1991), in the previously referenced I/O handbook chapter on recruitment, and Breaugh (1992), in his book *Recruitment: Science and Practice,* offered similar definitions of recruitment. Rynes (1991) defined recruitment as "encompass(ing) all organizational practices and decisions that affect either the number, or types, of individuals who are willing to apply for, or to accept, a given vacancy" (p. 429). Breaugh (1992) stated that "Employee recruitment involves those organizational activities that (1) influence the number and/or types of applicants who apply for a position and/or (2) affect whether a job offer is accepted" (p. 4).

Both of these definitions are quite broad in that they permit any organizational practice to be classified as recruitment and do not restrict our attention to traditional recruitment functions, such as designing brochures and advertisements or conducting campus interviews. Unfortunately, they also both confuse the recruitment *process* with recruitment *outcomes*. By stating that recruitment activities are those that influence recruitment outcomes, these definitions leave room for some rather odd interpretations. For example, a recruiting program (e.g., a new videotape, or a live information session) that failed to have any effect on applicant attitudes or behaviors would not be considered part of recruitment. Most of us (including Rynes and Breaugh, I suspect) would consider these *ineffective* recruitment programs, but recruitment programs just the same. Similarly, an organizational practice that had the unintended effect of "turning off" potential applicants (which might range from drug testing procedures perceived by applicants as an invasion of privacy, to public relations fiascoes, such as the Exxon Valdez incident) would be categorized as part of recruitment! As a result, such definitions obscure an important bit of reality: Recruitment objectives are often influenced by factors outside the traditional recruitment function.

Rynes and Barber (1990) addressed this problem by explicitly differentiating attraction from recruitment. They argued that recruitment practices were but one means of attracting applicants to organizations, thereby separating process from outcome. They identified modification of job inducements (when done for the purpose of attracting applicants) and identification of alternative applicant pools as other means of influencing attraction. By excluding these two approaches from their definition of recruitment, they clearly took a more restrictive approach than Rynes (1991) or Breaugh (1992), and there is some sentiment that their definition is too restrictive (e.g., Breaugh, 1992).

To avoid defining recruitment in terms of its consequences yet still maintain the breadth of the definitions offered by Rynes and Breaugh, I adopt the following definition: *Recruitment includes those practices and activities carried on by the organization with the primary purpose of identifying and attracting potential employees.*

This definition distinguishes recruitment practices and activities from their outcomes, identification and attraction. The primary objective of recruitment is to attract future employees. To do this, an appropriate pool of potential applicants must first be identified. Recruitment activities, then, are intended to help locate potential applicants and persuade them to pursue, and ultimately accept, employment with the organization.

The definition encompasses a wide range of organizational activities, from traditional recruitment functions, such as advertising and producing recruitment brochures, to modifications of the work environment (e.g. by creating alternative work schedules) when necessary to recruit new employees. Importantly, it focuses on those activities *intended* to influence recruitment outcomes, and in doing so recognizes that the correspondence between recruitment practices and recruitment outcomes is far from perfect. Few would argue that people pursue employment with companies, or choose to work for companies, on the basis of recruitment practices alone. Instead, these decisions are a function of some combination of recruitment and other forces.

Far from being irrelevant to the study of recruitment, these other factors can set boundaries for the role that recruitment can play in the identification and attraction of employees. For example, recruitment may have little effect when jobs are exceptionally attractive or exceptionally unattractive. Furthermore, some factors not initially considered in a recruitment strategy can *become* part of recruitment if circumstances so dictate. For example, a firm that learns its benefits package has made it less competitive in attracting future employees may modify that package to have greater applicant appeal, thereby making benefits part of recruitment.

This latter point reflects an important difference between my definition of recruitment and past definitions. In the past, recruitment was seen as the "medium" by which information about job attributes (the "message") was conveyed (Schwab, 1982). Indeed, for many years scholars attempted to separate medium and message. To the extent that organizations can and do alter job characteristics to attract employees, this separation may have led us to seriously underestimate the effects of recruitment programs.

Key Dimensions of Recruitment

Before we can identify critical research questions for recruitment, we first need a detailed understanding of recruitment and its elements. Recruitment is a complex process. Indeed, most criticisms of existing recruitment research suggest that it does not adequately capture the complexity of recruitment as it occurs in the real world. For instance, Rynes and Barber (1990) stated that "in most cases existing studies are extremely simplistic when evaluated against real-world attraction complexities. In particular, most studies have examined single strategies and limited dependent variables at single phases of the attraction process" (p. 305).

What then are the key dimensions of recruitment? What issues would a sufficiently complex model of recruitment include? Five dimensions of recruitment can be identified from the literature: *players, activities, outcomes, context* and *phases*. In this section, these dimensions and their elements are described, and some very general remarks are made about the way these dimensions have been employed in existing recruitment research.[1]

Players

This category refers to individuals or organizations playing a role in recruitment. Relevant players can either influence, or be influenced by, recruitment processes.

The primary players in recruitment are the organization that is engaged in recruitment and the applicant (or potential applicant) being recruited. As noted earlier, recruitment is an organizational function that depends on its ability to influence individuals (i.e., applicants or potential applicants). The organization acts and the recruit reacts. Both parties are critical to the matching process that ultimately leads to employment.

Between these two primary players, significantly more research has focused on the applicant perspective than on the organizational perspective. For example, many studies have examined applicant reactions to recruitment practices or factors influencing individual job choice decisions. This emphasis can be justified in that it is the decisions of applicants (or potential applicants) that, in aggregate, determine the effectiveness of recruitment. Within this category, however, some have argued that we have focused too heavily on specific types of applicants, limiting our understanding of the effect of recruitment on other types of applicants. In particular, Wanous and Colella (1989) lamented the overemphasis on recent college graduates in job choice research, noting that "the close proximity of students to researchers has proven to be an irresistible temptation" (p. 90). Although this problem is more severe with respect to some topics than others, it is certainly appropriate to be concerned about whether the applicants we study reflect the full range of potential applicants being recruited by organizations.

Relatively less attention has been paid to recruitment as viewed by the organization. This is unfortunate, as the relevance of our research is to a large degree dependent on how well we understand the organizational environment in which recruitment takes place. Appropriate questions would include how recruitment strategies are developed within organizations, what consequences these strategies are intended to have, and how they influence those and other organizational consequences. There is little empirical work at this level, and much of what exists focuses primarily on large firms. There is much room for additional research in this area (Rynes & Barber, 1990; Taylor & Giannantonio, 1993) and a need to ensure that the work that *is* done adequately represents the population of organizations involved in recruitment.

In addition to these primary players, there are other parties involved in recruitment, and their issues have been studied only rarely. We can categorize these other parties into two groups: organizational agents and outsiders.

Organizational agents are those individuals (or groups of individuals) who actually carry out or are responsible for the recruitment function. They might be internal to the organization (e.g., recruitment department) or external (e.g., advertising agency, headhunter). It is important to keep in mind that in reality organizations per se do not make decisions about recruitment or carry out recruitment activities; rather, individuals (or groups of individuals) act in the organization's behalf. This distinction is important inasmuch as agency theory (e.g., Eisenhart, 1989) suggests that one cannot merely assume that organizational agents are acting in the organizations' best interests.

Finally, so-called *outsiders* can play a role in recruitment, in that they too may react to the process. There is a significant "public relations" aspect to recruitment. During the recruitment process, organizations put forth various kinds of information about themselves. Some of this information is disseminated broadly (e.g. through advertisements in popular media), and therefore can influence public perceptions of the organization directly. Other information is gathered by applicants and, though not available to the general public, this information may be shared with the applicants' colleagues, friends, and relatives. These influences on outsiders could potentially influence the organization either by changing the behavior of potential consumers and investors or by changing the perceived attractiveness of the company to potential future applicants. Rynes and Barber (1990) referred to these consequences as a form of "spillover".

In summary, the number of players involved in the recruitment process is larger than typically conceived. In reviewing the recruitment literature, both Breaugh (1992) and Rynes, Heneman, and Schwab

(1980) suggested that recruitment research should focus on a greater variety of actors. This recommendation can apply both to the types of actors studied (e.g. more attention to actors other than the applicant or potential applicant) and to the types of individuals studied within categories (e.g. experienced versus entry-level applicants). In addition, Taylor and Giannantonio (1993) noted that few studies simultaneously investigate issues relevant to multiple actors, and called for researchers to develop a more interactionist perspective with respect to recruitment issues.

Activities

Recruitment activities are the specific tasks, procedures, and actions undertaken for purposes of recruitment. They are what the actors involved in recruitment (on the organization's behalf) actually *do*. Activities can be classified as *definition of the target population, choice of medium or source, message delivery, making the offer,* and *general administrative issues.*

Definition of the labor market refers to decisions regarding where to recruit (e.g., whether to conduct a local or national recruitment campaign), as well as which segment of the labor market to tap within a specific geographic region. For example, organizations might focus on potential applicants with specific educational backgrounds or skills (e.g., college graduates only), or might attempt to gain a competitive edge by focusing on market segments in which alternative employment opportunities might be limited (e.g., retirees, working parents, individuals with certain disabilities).

Choice of medium, or source, refers to the method used to reach the targeted population. Potential applicants can be reached through a variety of sources: word-of-mouth, employee referrals, job fairs, advertisements, employment agencies, and so on. Employers generally cannot use all possible sources, and decisions regarding which source to use may have consequences for both the type and the number of applicants who can be reached.

Message delivery refers to the dissemination of information through the selected sources. Message delivery can vary along several dimensions, including the nature of the message (e.g., whether information offered will be primarily positive or more realistic), the nature of the messenger (e.g., who will serve as the organization's spokesperson), and the timing of the message (e.g., whether the organization will stick to a specific recruitment cycle, whether it will attempt to reach applicants early or late in markets that have defined hiring cycles).

Making the offer refers to preparation of the final job offer for applicants who pass selection criteria. This activity includes decisions regarding job attributes that are malleable for purposes of recruitment (e.g., what the entry pay level will be), as well as procedural issues, such as how long the applicant has to decide on the offer and the degree to which elements of the offer package (e.g. salary, relocation expenses) are negotiable.

General administrative procedures refers to policies and practices for managing the overall recruitment function. These procedures have either an internal (organizational) or external (applicant) focus. Relevant procedures from the internal perspective would include performance management of those involved in recruitment (e.g., training and feedback provided) as well as procedures used to evaluate recruitment effectiveness. Applicant-directed activities would include issues such as how applicants are notified of the status of their application (e.g., how promptly and by what means) and how applicants are reimbursed for their recruitment-related expenses.

With respect to the current state of research, both Rynes and Barber (1990) and Rynes et al. (1980) argued that recruitment research should incorporate a greater variety of recruitment activities. To date, there has been a large number of studies of the effects of different recruitment sources, reactions to specific types of recruiters, and the nature of the recruitment message (e.g. whether exclusively favorable or more realistic). Other topics are relatively unexplored. In addition, there is little research that incorporates multiple recruitment activities and, as a result, we know little about how different activities might interact.

Outcomes

As our earlier discussion suggested, the primary objective of recruitment is the identification and attraction of potential employees. These outcomes are by no means easy to define or assess. Organizations are interested in attracting certain *numbers* of potential employees who have certain specific *attributes*. In other words, attraction has both quantitative and qualitative dimensions (Rynes & Barber, 1990). Regarding quantity, recruitment is most efficient when the number of applicants attracted is neither too small nor too large. Small applicant pools give the employer few options regarding which applicants to hire. Very large applicant pools, however, place heavy burdens on the organization's administrative systems and are generally undesirable. Regarding quality, organizations may differ in terms of what characteristics, or what level of characteristics, they are seeking; thus "successful" recruitment is best defined in accordance with whatever qualities the organization had in mind.

Having delineated qualitative and quantitative dimensions of attraction, it is also important to note that attraction occurs throughout the recruitment process. Potential applicants must choose to apply to the organization, they must persist through the selection process, and they must accept jobs if offered. Thus attraction must be assessed at multiple stages.

Beyond attraction, much recruitment research has focused on distal outcomes, that is, on outcomes farther removed from the recruitment process itself. For instance, recruitment can influence the post-hire attitudes and behaviors (e.g., satisfaction, commitment, length of service) of recruits. It can also influence attitudes and behaviors of existing employees, potential applicants, and other relevant parties (investors, customers) through the sort of spillover effects identified above. All of these outcomes are relevant to understanding the effect that recruitment might have on organizations. Taken in aggregate, they can have an effect on higher-level organizational outcomes, such as productivity, profitability, or other measures of firm performance.

The above discussion emphasized organizational consequences. However, recruitment clearly has consequences for other parties. Perhaps most important, the job seeker's satisfaction with the decision he or she made is an outcome relevant to the quality of worklife he or she experiences, and is therefore important above and beyond any possible organizational benefits that accrue from having more satisfied employees. In addition, organizational agents involved in recruitment may experience important outcomes related to their professional success, their ability to meet hidden agendas through recruitment, or both.

Rynes (1991) and Rynes and Barber (1990) argued that recruitment research should consider a greater variety of outcome variables. More specifically, Wanous and Colella (1989) recommended more attention to proximal as opposed to distal criteria. This recommendation is addressed in more detail below.

Context

Recruitment does not occur in a vacuum. Rather, it occurs in a real-world context in which a host of factors can influence both the kinds of recruitment activities organizations choose to engage in and applicants' responses to those activities. Context factors can be classified as either external or internal. External factors include aspects of the environment outside the recruiting organization. The state of the labor market is one such factor. The availability of applicants relative to the availability of jobs clearly fluctuates over time. From the organization's standpoint, different strategies may well be in order in tight versus loose markets. From the individuals' perspective, responses (especially behavioral responses) to recruitment may be constrained when few jobs are available. Legislation is another important external factor: Organizations' decisions regarding recruitment are constrained by existing employment law, particularly those laws dealing with employment discrimination and affirmative action.

Internal context factors primarily focus on characteristics of the organization itself, such as its business strategy (type of employees needed, relative importance of human capital), its economic position (ability to pay), and its attractiveness to potential applicants. These factors may constrain the recruitment options available to organizations, and also may modify the importance of recruitment as a means of attracting potential employees.

Rynes and her colleagues have repeatedly called for greater attention to the context in which recruitment occurs (Rynes, 1991; Rynes & Barber, 1990; Rynes, Heneman, & Schwab, 1980; Schwab, 1982). This attention can take two forms. One might either empirically assess recruitment issues across a variety of contexts, or one might study recruitment in a single context, taking care to clarify the context so that others will be able to understand the exact circumstances under which particular effects were or were not found. In recent years, there has been some progress along the lines of the latter approach but very little along the lines of the former.

Phases

There is widespread recognition that the recruitment process consists of multiple stages or phases, and there have been numerous calls for longitudinal research carried out across phases (e.g., Breaugh, 1992; Rynes, 1991; Rynes & Barber, 1990; Taylor & Giannantonio, 1993). However, little attention has been paid to the identification or delineation of those stages. Clearly, initial application is a different phase from job offer acceptance, but it is difficult to say with much more precision than that how many phases there might be, or when one phase ends and the next begins.

One approach to systematic delineation of phases draws from Boudreau and Rynes's (1985) classification of (potential) employees as they move through the recruitment/job search process. They identify three classifications that might be useful markers of transitions from one phase to another: *applicant population, applicant pool,* and *selectees.* The *applicant population* is the group from which the organization can recruit given the choices it has made regarding recruitment (e.g., decisions to target a particular segment of the labor market or to use a particular source). The *applicant pool* consists of those individuals from the applicant population who choose to apply to the organization. Finally, *selectees* are those individuals from the applicant pool who are actually offered employment.

These categories can be used to define stages or phases of recruitment by asserting that when individuals move from one category to another, they have moved into a new phase of recruitment. Using this approach, the first phase of recruitment would involve outreach to an applicant population in an attempt to persuade some portion of that population to apply for positions, that is, to become applicants. Phase 2 would consist of attempts to persuade applicants to remain interested in the organization and to continue to pursue the job opportunity until the point at which they either become or fail to become selectees. In Phase 3, organizations would attempt to persuade selectees to accept job offers and become new hires. It should be noted that these phases themselves can stretch out over (sometimes extended) periods of time, and that there may be room for longitudinal designs even within phases. These rough distinctions between phases, however, can be useful in organizing existing recruitment literature and structuring future recruitment research.

Using the Key Dimensions to Organize and Evaluate Recruitment Research

The above discussion of recruitment dimensions introduced a large number of variables relevant to recruitment research. They are summarized in Table 1.1. Perusal of reviews of the recruitment literature (Breaugh, 1992; Rynes, 1991; Rynes & Barber, 1990; Rynes, Heneman, & Schwab, 1980; Schwab, 1982; Taylor & Giannantonio, 1993; Wanous & Colella, 1989) reveals that recruitment experts have called for future research that incorporates "more" of each of these elements: more actors, more activities, more outcomes, more context, more phases. In the context of designing individual studies, such calls can be overwhelming and, indeed, depressing, as it is highly unlikely that all (or even many) of the elements of these five dimensions can be examined within a single design. The framework provided in Figure 1 is far more useful as a means of identifying areas where current knowledge is rich or poor. I rely on these key dimensions in two ways in organizing the material that follows. First, as noted below, I have chosen one of the dimensions (phases) to provide the overall structure of subsequent chapters. Second, I return to these dimensions in the final chapter, as a means of assessing the current state of knowledge and of recommending directions for future research.

Structure of Remaining Chapters

In the chapters that follow, I use the three recruitment phases described above to organize the rather vast and diverse literature on recruitment. One advantage of delineating recruitment into these three stages is that each stage has unique characteristics that can be used to identify and differentiate appropriate research questions. Phase 1, which involves the identification and generation of applicants (from the organization's perspective) or job opportunities (from the individual's perspective), can be characterized as a phase of *extensive search*." During this phase, organizations seek to reduce a large applicant population to a narrower applicant pool, from which a subset of individuals will ultimately be pursued for hire. Relatively little information about each applicant is sought at this phase. On the contrary, the applicant population from which applicants are drawn is largely faceless until the end of the phase, when they become actual applicants. Similarly, most applicants attempt to generate multiple job opportunities during phase one and may know relatively little about the jobs for which they apply. In addition, they may have had no personal contact at all with the organization at this point. Thus, the first phase is characterized by (1) *screening* as opposed to final *choice*, (2) limited information about multiple possibilities, and (3) little, if any, interpersonal contact.

During the second phase of recruitment, the pool of applicants is narrowed to a group of selectees (individuals who have received job offers). This phase is better characterized as one of *intensive search*. Having narrowed down the options during phase one, organizations and applicants search for in-depth information about the remaining subset of opportunities. During this phase, interpersonal relationships between applicants and the organization (more specifically,

Table 1.1   Key Dimensions of Recruitment

ACTORS:
    Individual/applicant
    Organization
    Organizational agents
    Outsiders

ACTIVITIES:
    Defining target population
    Choice of medium/source
    Message delivery
    Closing the deal
    Administrative processes

OUTCOMES:
    Attraction
    Post-hire
    Organizational performance
    Other

CONTEXT:
    Internal
    External

PHASES:
    Generating applicants
    Maintaining applicant status
    Job choice

representatives of the organization) are established. In addition, it is at the end of this phase that the organization makes its choice regarding whom to hire. Thus, Phase 2 is characterized by (1) personal contact, (2) a search for detailed information, and (3) on the part of the employer, a final choice.

In Phase 3, the selectee decides whether to accept the offer of employment. Again, this stage is one of intensive information seeking. It is also characterized by choice (accepting a single job and rejecting all others) rather than screening (narrowing a large pool down to a smaller subset). As a result, this phase may be taken more seriously by applicants, as a decision to accept one job effectively eliminates alternative opportunities, at least in the short run.

The unique characteristics of these distinct phases suggest that it may make sense to review literature relevant to each stage separately. Therefore, Chapters 2, 3, and 4 deal with individual phases in chronological order. Chapter 2 addresses the phase of recruitment in which potential applicants become applicants, Chapter 3 addresses the phase in which applicants become selectees, and Chapter 4 addresses the phase in which selectees become employees. To the extent that it is possible to do so, I also organize material within chapters chronologically, that is, in the order in which the events they describe occur within the recruitment process.

Chapter 5 departs somewhat from this pattern, in that it deals with recruitment's overall impact on organizational outcomes. Consideration of this question requires consideration of multiple phases of recruitment. Relatively few studies have taken this broader perspective, and the chapter makes specific recommendations for conducting additional research along these lines.

Each chapter provides a review of existing literature and recommendations for future research. In choosing literature for review, I have attempted to provide the reader with a clear sense of how research on different topics has developed over the years, but at the same time have tried not to be overly redundant with existing reviews (e.g., Breaugh, 1992; Rynes, 1991; Rynes & Barber, 1990; Rynes, Heneman, & Schwab, 1980; Schwab, 1982; Taylor & Giannantonio, 1993; Wanous & Colella, 1989). Therefore recent studies typically receive more detailed attention than earlier studies, particularly if the topic is one that has been extensively reviewed.

The final chapter (Chapter 6) returns to the question, "What should we do next?" In this chapter, I summarize the strengths and weaknesses of existing research and propose a set of guidelines for prioritizing future research.

NOTE

1. This section is based in large part on a number of reviews and critiques of the recruitment literature: Breaugh (1992), Rynes (1991), Rynes & Barber (1990), Rynes, Heneman, & Schwab (1980), Schwab (1982), Schwab, Rynes, & Aldag (1987), Taylor & Giannantonio (1993), and Wanous & Colella (1989). Each provides a slightly different focus or perspective, but all were very helpful in assessing key aspects of recruitment as well as the current state of research.

2 Generating Applicants

This chapter examines research and research needs relevant to the earliest stage of recruitment: the generation of applicants. During this stage, an applicant population (a relatively large and broadly defined population of potential applicants) becomes an applicant pool (a comparatively smaller group of specific individuals who have actually applied for a job). As noted earlier, this stage involves what is called *extensive search*: applicants and employers are engaged in generating large numbers of candidates for future consideration. The applicant attempts to generate a pool of opportunities from which one (eventually) will be chosen. The employer attempts to generate a pool of applicants from which some subset will be selected for hire. Because each player is potentially dealing with a large number of candidates at this point, the amount of information sought on each may be fairly limited. In addition, interactions between organization and potential applicant at this stage are largely faceless and impersonal. This stage culminates with formation of an applicant pool, the aggregated result of individual applicants' decision to apply or not apply for a position.

Key outcomes for this stage are those directly related to formation of an applicant pool: the identification and attraction of potential applicants. The recruitment process must identify individuals who will meet the organization's needs (in terms of qualifications, demographic characteristics, or other characteristics relevant to organizational objectives). Furthermore, those individuals must be persuaded to pursue employment with the organization in sufficient numbers to meet the organization's hiring objectives, but the number of applicants should not be so great as to overburden the organization's ability to efficiently process applications.

In addition to these immediate outcomes, actions taken during this stage of recruitment can also be related to post-hire outcomes, such as performance and turnover. Also, because organizations communicate extensively in order to identify potential applicants, the possibility that these practices will result in spillover effects (i.e., that they will influence the attitudes and behaviors of those not currently in the targeted applicant population) is strong.

This chapter reviews what we know, and also points out what we don't know, about this first stage of recruitment. It begins from the organization's perspective, examining organizational decisions regarding the targeting of applicant populations and the choice of recruitment sources. It then shifts to the applicant's perspective, focusing on how potential applicants form initial impressions of organizations, how they react to recruitment materials, and how they make decisions regarding whether or not to pursue employment with a firm. Within each section, topics are addressed in chronological order, that is, in the order in which they must be dealt with by the actors involved. Finally, spillover effects are discussed.

As the subsequent sections make clear, there are many unanswered questions pertaining to this initial stage of recruitment, particularly with respect to the primary objectives of identification and attraction. This is unfortunate, as these initial activities and decisions create the foundation for later recruitment, selection, and job choice. An applicant or job opportunity that is discarded at this early phase surely is just as lost as if it is discarded later. Part of the reason for the shortage of studies in this area may be methodological. Many of the issues that need to be addressed will require different sampling and data collection strategies from those that have typically been employed by recruitment researchers. The final section of this chapter addresses this point.

Organizational Issues in Applicant Generation

Deciding Whom to Target

One of the first recruitment decisions made by the organization is whom to target as potential applicants. Few organizations have the resources, the desire, or the need to contact all possible applicants. A reasonable alternative approach would be to narrow the focus of recruitment to specific applicant groups likely to yield candidates who meet the organization's requirements and also are likely to be interested in the opportunities the organization has to offer. Yet we know little about how, or whether, organizations make systematic and effective applicant targeting decisions. There is a great need for better understanding of why and how these choices are made, what their consequences are, and by what process(es) these consequences are obtained.

Geographic Targeting

One dimension of applicant targeting involves the geographic boundaries of the recruitment process. Common wisdom suggests that higher-level jobs require broader searches than lower-level jobs. For example, one might search nationally or even world-wide for a chief executive officer but restrict search to the local labor market for janitorial staff. This approach is driven by a balance of cost and availability. It is generally the case that organizations can hire sufficient numbers of lower-level employees from local labor markets, with relatively low recruitment costs and without incurring employee relocation costs. For higher-job levels, however, organizations may be unable to find needed personnel in the local labor market and may therefore have to conduct more expensive regional or national recruitment.

Unfortunately, there has been virtually no systematic study of the rationale for, or consequences of, geographic boundaries in recruitment. This is unfortunate given the importance of geographic location to applicants. A number of studies suggest that applicants "rule out" jobs located outside their preferred geographic area (e.g., Barber & Roehling, 1993; Osborn, 1990; Rynes & Lawler, 1983). All three of these studies used college students as subjects, suggesting that the importance of location is not limited to low-level employees. And many authors have noted increasing resistance among organizational employees of all levels to accept jobs that require relocation (e.g., Turban, Campion, & Eyring, 1995; Noe & Barber, 1993). Thus there may well be a connection between the geographic boundaries of recruitment and successful attraction of applicants, with recruitment being more effective when it focuses on applicants likely to consider the organization's location attractive. In addition to this attraction effect, research on relocation indicates that feelings about the location in which one works may have post-hire consequences: Pinder (1977, 1989) found that relocated employees who preferred their new location showed greater post-transfer satisfaction than other relocated employees.

How might geographic boundaries of recruitment be drawn to maximize employee attraction and subsequent satisfaction? One approach would be to limit recruitment to the area in which the job is located (presuming that those already in the area have a preference for that area). Another approach would be to identify other geographic areas that are similar to the organization's location in terms of city size, climate, recreational opportunities, and so forth. Such targeting could have advantages both pre- and post-hire. Research on attitudes toward relocation (e.g., Carruthers & Pinder, 1983; Noe & Barber, 1993) has indicated that individuals hold preferences for communities with specific characteristics, and that they are more willing to relocate to areas that offer those characteristics. Thus they may be more easily attracted. In addition, research on the consequences of relocation suggests that stress and anxiety decrease, and adjustments are more easily made, when people relocate to new communities that are similar to their former homes (Brett, Stroh, & Reilly, 1992; Pinder & Schroeder, 1987). Despite these possible advantages, there has been little attention within the recruitment literature to geographic issues.

Targeting Applicant Types

A second dimension of targeted recruitment involves focusing on applicants with specific characteristics. Of course, organizations should target those individuals who have the skills and abilities required to effectively perform the job. Yet for many organizations (and for many jobs) it is likely that qualified individuals can be located in many different applicant subgroups. Furthermore, as Rynes and Barber (1990) argued, skill requirements may be more malleable than they might initially appear, as they can be changed by redesigning jobs. Therefore employers may have a great deal of latitude in choosing what type of applicant to target. Again, from an attraction standpoint it makes sense to identify those individuals who are qualified to do the job and who are likely to accept a job offer should they receive one.

The most extensive discussion of applicant targeting that exists in the literature appears in Rynes and Barber (1990). Their primary argument is based on relative demand for workers in certain groups. They suggested that organizations can gain a competitive edge in recruitment by focusing on candidates generally overlooked by other employers. They place special emphasis on "nontraditional" applicants (i.e., applicants who are different from typical hires in terms of age, educational background, gender, etc.) who are ignored despite their potential productivity. Yet it might also be recognized that in some cases it can be advantageous for organizations to focus on "nontraditional" applicants who, in fact, have lower skills and abilities than others, if the job circumstances (e.g., jobs in highly mechanistic environments) dictate that such individuals can be hired at little risk to the organization.

Rynes and Barber argued that shifts to "nontraditional" applicant pools are most likely when applicant shortages are large; when jobs are unattractive and the organization is unable to pay high wages; when the jobs being filled do not lead directly to higher level organization jobs; when skill levels are flexible; and when organizations are stable and structured along mechanistic lines. In such scenarios, the need for alternative recruitment procedures is high, and the risks associated with appealing to alternative applicant pools are relatively low.

Rynes and Barber also suggested that changes in targeted applicant populations may require or facilitate changes in other recruitment procedures. For example, focusing on applicants who are not in high demand may permit organizations to lower their hiring wages. It might at the same time require modification of recruitment messages and materials to ensure that nontraditional applicants are comfortable joining the organization.

As was the case with geographic targeting, there is essentially no empirical evidence regarding decisions to target specific applicant groups. We know little about whether, why, or when organizations actually target alternative populations. We know little about the consequences of such targeting, either in the short term (consequences for attraction) or in the long run (post-hire consequences). We can offer little advice regarding effective approaches to targeting nontraditional groups. Clearly, this is an area where additional research is needed.

Choice of Recruitment Source

Having identified its target population of applicants, the organization must now choose the source or sources by which those potential applicants will be reached. Traditional sources include employee referrals, employment agencies (including campus placement offices and executive search firms), newspaper or radio advertisements, and unsolicited applications or "walk-ins." More recently, organizations have turned to alternative sources, such as on-line (internet) hiring services, job fairs, and competitors' layoffs/outsourcing programs as means of identifying candidates (Glickstein & Ramer, 1988).

The effectiveness of different recruitment sources is one of the most intensely researched aspects of recruitment. Ironically, this stream of research has little to say about the primary outcomes of recruitment: the identification and attraction of applicants. When these outcomes are mentioned at all, it is typically in the context of explaining more distal outcomes, such as post-hire longevity, performance, absenteeism, or satisfaction. This section reviews existing research on recruitment source effects, and provides suggestions for future research directions.

Early Research on Source Effects

Early recruitment source studies were primarily descriptive in nature. For example, Gannon (1971) found that rehires, walk-ins, and referred applicants had lower turnover than applicants drawn from other sources (hiring agencies and newspaper ads). Similarly, Decker & Cornelius (1979) found that referrals tended to have long tenure and that applicants hired via newspaper ads and employment agencies tended to have the shortest tenure. Breaugh (1981) investigated the relationship of recruitment sources to a variety of outcome variables and found source effects for job performance, absenteeism, and work attitudes. Job performance was higher for those hired via ads in professional journals or convention materials and for those who initiated applications themselves, whereas performance of those hired via college placement and newspaper ads was relatively low. Absenteeism was relatively high among those hired via newspaper advertisements. Finally, those hired via college placement tended to have lower job involvement and lower satisfaction with supervision than those hired via other sources. It has generally been concluded that informal sources tend to outperform more formal recruitment sources.

Theoretical Rationales for Source Effects

Although early studies did not set out to test theoretical models of why recruitment might affect post-hire outcomes, such as turnover, performance, and attitudes, their authors, along with other recruitment scholars, did suggest a variety of reasons why these effects might have been obtained. For instance, Decker and Cornelius (1979) proposed that different recruiting sources might have different effects on applicants' perceptions of the ease of movement between jobs. Applicants who used a source that exposed them to numerous employment opportunities might be more likely to turn over later on, as their perception of the ability to find other employment might be higher. Breaugh (1981) proposed that applicants recruited from different sources might be treated differently following hire, and that these post-hire treatment differences might explain differences in post-hire outcomes. Breaugh (1981) also pointed out that the general pattern of recruitment source research suggested that informal sources led to superior post-hire outcomes. He drew from Wanous's (1978) work on realistic job previews to suggest that informal recruitment sources might provide more specific or more accurate information to job applicants, thus leading to greater role clarity, more realistic expectations, and better adjustment to the new job, which in turn would lead to better attitudes, performance, and greater longevity. Finally, Schwab (1982) proposed that recruitment sources might differ in the kind of applicants they reach, and that these differences in applicants might result in different post-hire outcomes.

Several studies were conducted for the purpose of testing these theoretical rationales for recruiting source effects. The bulk of the testing has focused on the latter two explanations: the realism of information hypothesis, and the individual differences hypothesis. In many cases, these perspectives have been pitted against one another as "competing" hypotheses. Unfortunately, the two hypotheses are not always equally well operationalized, making such comparative conclusions difficult.

Taylor and Schmidt (1983), using a sample of packaging plant employees, examined whether recruitment sources (referrals, newspaper ads, public employment office referrals, radio ads, rehires, television ads, walk-ins) differed in effectiveness in terms of attendance, performance, and tenure. Rehires showed significantly longer tenure and lower absenteeism than all other sources. No performance differences were found.

To test whether differences in applicant characteristics across recruitment sources might explain the observed turnover and absenteeism effects, Taylor and Schmidt assessed each new hire on a set of variables identified by management as related to employee success (e.g., height, weight, shift preference). Their analysis indicated that rehires (the most successful group of new hires) did differ significantly from all other groups on these characteristics, supporting the individual differences hypothesis. This is a particularly strong test of the hypothesis, as individual difference variables were chosen because of their anticipated relationship to relevant outcome variables.

Their study also provided some support for the realism hypothesis. Taylor and Schmidt proposed that informal sources (referrals and rehires), which are believed to provide better information than formal sources, would generate employees with better post-hire outcomes than formal sources (e.g., television advertisements, newspaper advertisements, employment agencies), which are believed to provide less information. This hypothesis was partially supported, as rehires (but not referrals) exceeded other groups with respect to tenure and absenteeism. It should be noted that information quality was presumed in this case, and not actually measured. However, a study by Quaglieri (1982) provided some support for Taylor & Schmidt's assumptions.

Breaugh and Mann (1984) similarly tested individual differences and realism as competing hypotheses. Using a sample of social service workers, they examined relationships between recruitment source (newspaper advertisement, direct application, and employee referral) and two outcome variables: performance and turnover. They found that direct applicants (those who initiated contact themselves) had higher performance and slightly better retention than applicants recruited via other sources. To examine the mechanisms underlying these results, they measured a set of individual difference characteristics (demographic variables, applicant quality, and perceived ease of movement) and also assessed new hires' retrospective impressions of how realistic their information was at the time they were hired. In support of the realism hypothesis, they found that direct applicants did have more realistic information than applicants in the other groups. Relatively less support was found for the individual differences hypothesis, as applicant quality and perceived ease of movement were not found to differ across sources.

Blau (1990) provided a third test of these competing hypotheses. Using a sample of bank tellers, he examined the relationship between recruitment sources (newspaper ads, employment agencies, walk-ins, and referrals) and employee performance. Results indicated that walkins (i.e., direct applicants) had higher performance than applicants recruited via other means. Blau also found that walk-ins had higher ability scores than applicants from other sources, supporting the individual differences hypothesis. (However, he found no differences in motivation to apply, as had been suggested in Breaugh & Mann, 1984). The realism hypothesis received less support, in that referrals, not walk-ins, had the most realistic information at time of hire (based on a retrospective measure also employed by Breaugh & Mann, 1984).

Williams, Labig, and Stone (1993) studied the processes underlying source effects in a sample of nurses. First, relationships between sources (referral, previous rotation/internship experience, rehires, campus visits, newspaper or other advertisements, and walk-ins) and two post-hire outcomes (turnover and performance) were investigated. Unfortunately, no significant source effects were found, preventing the authors from conducting meaningful direct tests for mediation. This outcome is particularly unfortunate, as this study included some design features that were superior to those used in previous studies. In particular, it is noteworthy that in this study, information realism was assessed at the time of hire and therefore is not subject to the kind of biases that might influence the retrospective reports used by Breaugh & Mann (1984) or Blau (1990). In addition, Williams et al. allowed for the possibility that applicants might use multiple recruitment sources (and found that approximately one third of their sample had used multiple sources). This approach seems substantially more realistic than the more typical approach of forcing subjects to identify and report a single recruitment source.

Despite the inability to use formal tests for mediation, Williams et al. (1993) were able to provide data suggestive of mediation effects. The recruitment sources did vary in terms of experience, providing some support for the individual differences model. In addition, there were differences in pre-hire information by source, providing some support for the realistic information model. However, the pattern of these information differences was not as simple as the informal/formal distinction often relied upon. They found that rehires, nurses hired following clinical rotations, and individuals using multiple recruitment sources had greater pre-hire knowledge than employee referrals, campus interviews, advertisements, or walk-ins.

Werbel and Landau (1996) tested three mediation hypotheses: the individual differences and information realism models, as well as a model based on the concept of person-job fit. This hypothesis suggests that certain sources (most notably, employee referral) provide the organization's agent with an opportunity to screen out applicants who are unlikely to be successful, resulting in better post-hire outcomes among those who are ultimately hired.

Werbel and Landau studied the relationship between recruitment sources (newspaper advertisements, self-initiated contact, corporate recruiters, referrals, and college placement) and two outcome variables (performance and turnover) in a sample of life insurance sales representatives. They found relatively weak source effects: sources were unrelated to turnover and only marginally related to performance, with only one significant contrast: Placement office hires tended to have better performance than employees hired via newspaper advertisements.

To test the mediating models, the authors collected data on demographic characteristics (age, education) as individual differences. They assessed information realism by comparing applicant expectations regarding the job with the opinions of current job incumbents (an improvement over previous operationalizations of realism, as it avoids retrospective report biases and addresses the actual realism of applicant expectations rather than applicant perceptions of the quality of their information). Finally, they assessed applicants' own impressions of how well suited they were for the job.

Werbel and Landau's (1996) data did not support any of the mediation models. There were no effects to be mediated with respect to turnover, and none of the proposed mediators were associated with performance, eliminating them as possible mediators of the source-performance relationship. They did not, however, find that age and education varied by source (with placement office hires being younger and better educated than other hires). Furthermore, realism varied by source, with referrals having somewhat less realistic expectations than did walk-ins or agency hires, a finding that contrasts with presumptions that referrals lead to realistic information. Finally, fit also differed by source, with referrals and self-initiated applicants perceiving better job fit.

Finally, Griffeth, Hom, Fink, and Cohen (1997) used structural equation models to simultaneously test for mediation effects associated with individual differences and with realism. In addition, these authors used a greater variety of indicators of realism than are typically employed, focusing not only on met expectations but also on role clarity and coping skills. Using a sample of 221 newly hired nurses, Griffeth et al. found that recruitment sources were associated with individual differences and also with realism. Only realism was significantly related to post-hire outcomes, however. Therefore, although recruitment source effects may be mediated through realism, they do not appear to be mediated through individual differences. In addition, Griffeth et al. (1997) provided evidence that recruitment sources had direct impact on post-hire consequences over and beyond the impact that could be explained through realism. As a result, they encouraged research into additional mediating processes.

Evaluation of tests of theoretical models. In general, the above research can be characterized as providing some (limited) support for both the individual differences and realism hypotheses. This is not in itself problematic, as the hypotheses are not mutually exclusive—both may be correct. What is more troublesome is that the operationalization of key mediating variables for either of these models is often inadequate. It is essential that future tests of the individual differences hypothesis clearly identify that individual characteristics are likely to be associated with the outcome of interest and also that are likely to differ across recruitment sources. Too often, the individual differences hypothesis is tested using a few demographic variables with no clear relationship to either performance or turnover, resulting in fairly weak tests of the theory. In addition, it is essential that tests of the realism hypothesis assess what applicants actually knew or believed about the job at the time of application. Retrospective measures and perceptual measures may be influenced by a host of biases that can weaken tests of this hypothesis.

A second concern is the relatively narrow focus of this research, which for the most part addresses only two possible hypotheses, individual differences and information realism. Though various authors have suggested hypotheses involving differences in motivation to apply or in labor market mobility across sources, these hypotheses have been tested only once each, and in each case have been dealt with as individual differences rather than as differences across sources. Furthermore, though Blau (1990) suggested that post-hire outcomes occur because people hired via different sources are treated differently post-hire, I found no empirical tests of this hypothesis.

How Robust are Recruitment Source Effects?

An interesting finding to be drawn from the research described above is how frequently the effect to be mediated is small, nonexistent, or inconsistent with earlier research. Taylor and Schmidt (1983) failed to find performance differences, and did not find referrals to be a superior source with respect to tenure or absenteeism. Breaugh and Mann (1984) found performance effects but only small retention results. Again, retention failed to "fit the pattern," as referrals had lower retention than direct applicants. Blau (1990) found performance effects, but direct hires were superior to referrals. Williams et al. (1993) failed to find effects for turnover or performance. Werbel and Landau (1996) found a significant relationship for turnover (although, again, referrals failed to outperform other sources), and only weak results for performance.

These difficulties in replicating earlier findings raise the question of whether it is appropriate to continue to try to explain a phenomenon which might not exist! It may be more appropriate at this point to consider why anticipated source effects are not always observed. Several recent studies have looked at contingency factors that might help clarify this mixed bag of results.

Three studies assessed whether observed relationships between recruitment sources and post-hire outcomes were consistent across demographic groups. Caldwell and Spivey (1983) found race-related effects with respect to turnover: Employee referrals were the best source of long-tenure employees for whites, whereas employment agencies were the best source of long-tenure employees among blacks. Kirnan, Farley, and Geisinger (1989) found significant differences in source use by race and gender, with females and blacks more inclined to use formal sources than their male non-minority counterparts. However, they found that recruiting source was unrelated to performance for any group and had little impact on turnover. Consistent with earlier research, applicants hired via informal sources tended to have somewhat greater longevity. Finally, Vecchio (1995), using a national sample to study relationships between recruitment source and work attitudes, found differences in source use by income and education (higher for applicants identified by recruiters, lower for walk-ins). He also found differences by gender (relatively more men were hired via recruiters and relatively more women were hired via newspaper advertisements) and race (relatively more non-whites were hired via recruiters and relatively more whites were hired via walk-ins and employment agencies). He found no relationship, however, between recruitment source and job attitudes.

Future Directions for Source Research

Again, these recent studies fail to paint a compelling picture regarding relationships between recruitment source and post-hire outcomes. How should recruitment scholars respond to this pattern of findings? There are really two issues here: How can we best make sense of existing, and conflicting, findings regarding relationships between recruitment sources and post-hire outcomes? And, are we addressing the most pressing and most appropriate research questions regarding recruitment source?

With respect to the first issue, one important step would be to use meta-analysis as a means of identifying the true relationship between recruitment sources and post-hire consequences. Meta-analysis is a statistical technique that accumulates results across studies, correcting for statistical artifacts and therefore generating more accurate estimates of relationships. Unfortunately, efforts to conduct such an analysis of the recruitment source literature is hampered by the fact that there are relatively few studies that use the same dependent (outcome) and independent (source) variables. This suggests that recruitment source researchers should focus on studies that replicate the dependent and independent variables used in existing research, so that ultimately the recruitment source literature can be subjected to meta-analysis.

An alternative approach would be to reconsider the kinds of research questions we address in studying recruitment sources. Current research focuses on post-hire consequences and largely ignores the impact that recruitment sources have on more immediate recruitment issues. Several recruitment source scholars have concluded that this focus is inappropriate. For example, Williams et al. (1993) wrote that

(w)e believe it would be worthwhile to redirect the focus of recruitment source research toward pre-hire outcomes. Although scant research has been conducted, Boudreau & Rynes's (1985) utility model clearly demonstrates that even small changes in the level and variability of applicant qualification, the number of applicants, and the rate of job acceptance can have large effects on the payoff that organizations derive from selection systems. (p. 172)

Williams et al. (1993) also made a compelling argument about the shortcomings of using recruitment source data to study turnover. Specifically, they pointed out that this approach ignores the host of other potential influences on turnover, and therefore suffers from considerable omitted variable bias. Thus they suggested that it is appropriate to examine recruitment sources as influences on immediate recruitment outcomes, and inappropriate (given typical research designs) to examine their influence on post-hire consequences. Werbel and Landau (1996) concurred with this view:

> Future research evaluating the effectiveness of any recruitment source should consider the purpose of recruitment, generating a pool of job applicants who meet minimum job qualifications. Thus, one should evaluate the effectiveness of recruitment by using criteria, such as the number of applicants considered and percentage of applicants who meet minimum job qualifications. Post-hire effectiveness is more likely to be affected by selection, training, and socialization practices than by recruitment sources. (pp. 1348-1349).

One way to resolve the question of whether recruitment source studies should focus on immediate or longer-term outcomes is to incorporate the practitioner point of view. The applied value of recruitment source research depends on the extent to which scholars and managers use the same yardstick to evaluate effectiveness. Unfortunately, I was not able to find data describing managerial expectations for recruitment sources. Descriptive reports of managerial preferences for particular sources are not difficult to find (e.g., Bureau of National Affairs, 1988; Terpstra, 1996), but these reports typically do not indicate *why* one source is preferred over another, that is, what criteria are being used to establish effectiveness. In the absence of such data, I am persuaded by the arguments of Williams et al. (1993) and Werbel and Landau (1996) and suggest that future research on recruitment sources should focus on the *identification* and *attraction* of applicants.

Regarding identification, researchers might examine whether a particular source identifies reasonable numbers of applicants meeting the organization's criteria. The phrase *reasonable numbers* acknowledges that it is possible to have too many applicants, raising the cost and reducing the efficiency of the recruitment process. Though rarely addressed in the academic literature, the cost-effectiveness of recruitment sources is a criterion of interest to practitioners (Glickstein & Ramer, 1988), and can have significant impact on estimates of selection utility (e.g., Martin & Raju, 1992; Law & Myors, 1993). The phrase *meets the organization's criteria* recognizes that basic ability to do the job might not be the only criterion of interest to organizations. For example, organizations may seek a particular demographic mix of employees, either in a voluntary attempt to build a diverse workforce or in response to governmental pressures. Fortunately, some of the existing recruitment source literature sheds light on these issues. Several studies found differences in source use by different demographic groups (Kirnan, et al., 1989; Vecchio, 1995), suggesting that some sources are more useful than others in identifying applicants with specific characteristics. In addition, the variation across sources in applicant quality and in selection ratios observed by Kirnan et al. (1989) and Williams et al. (1993) suggests that some sources are more likely to generating "hirable" candidates than others.

Regarding attraction, the question is whether potential applicants contacted via a particular source are likely to react favorably to the contact. For example, it has long been believed that newspaper advertisements are unlikely to provide good leads for upper-level positions (Kelley, 1993), which may cause some applicants to disregard this source. In addition, if applicants recruited through different sources are treated differently during the selection process (Breaugh, 1981), they may show greater persistence in pursuing the job. For instance, recruits who feel they are "sponsored" by a recruiter or by a friend who works for the organization may be less likely to withdraw than recruits who do not perceive any personal connection. Though no studies have directly examined these issues, Kirnan et al. (1992) provided some evidence relevant to the second question. They observed different withdrawal rates across sources, with higher withdrawal for newspaper ads, school placement, and manager referrals, and lower withdrawal for employee referrals. Additional research along these lines would be enlightening.

Research into the relationship between recruitment sources and recruitment outcomes should consider not only what happens but why it happens. For example, do persistence effects occur because people initially contacted through different sources are treated differently as they go through the hiring process? Do referrals receive more social support? Are campus placement office recruits supported and encouraged by their campus recruiter? Or does persistence vary because applicants using certain sources generate more opportunities and thus are more likely to decline a particular offer? There is much room for improvement in our understanding of these questions, and perhaps this is where recruitment sources researchers should focus their efforts.

Applicant Issues: The Decision to Apply

Having identified and chosen appropriate target populations and recruitment sources, the recruiting organization must now set out to persuade individuals to apply to the organization. Typically, the organization will communicate information about the specific job and the organization itself through specific media (ads, internet postings, placement office postings) in an attempt to persuade potential employees to become applicants. This section examines what we know about individual reactions to these early recruitment efforts.

Early Impressions: Organizational Image

Real-world applicants do not start out as "blank slates" from a recruitment standpoint; rather, they often have some impression of employing organizations even before they are exposed to recruitment materials. These general impressions have been referred to as organizational images and are expected to be related to the organization's ability to attract applicants (e.g., Fombrun & Shanley, 1990; Stigler, 1962). Though there have been calls for increased attention to the role image plays in recruitment (e.g., Rynes, 1991), as yet there has been little empirical work on this topic.

Image Defined

An important starting point is to define what exactly is meant by the term *organizational image.* Within the recruitment literature, Tom (1971) has provided the most comprehensive definition. He described image in general terms, as the way people perceive an organization and, in more specific terms as a loose structure of knowledge, beliefs and feelings about an organization. This notion of image as a total impression based on a loose combination of facts and feelings is reiterated in the definitions of other image scholars outside the recruitment field (e.g., marketing; Dichter, 1985; Golden, Albaum, & Zimmer, 1987). It is also consistent with other definitions employed in the recruitment literature. For example, Gatewood, Gowan, and Lautenschlager (1993) defined image as a general reaction to an organization's name, and Belt and Paolillo (1982) defined corporate image as a "set of attributes which can be perceived about a particular firm and may be induced from the way that firm deals with its employees, clients or customers, and society" (p. 107).

According to Tom, image may be vague or clear, weak or strong. It may vary from person to person and can change over time. Most other definitions have not been as specific in discussing variations in image. However, Leister and Maclachlan (1975) suggested that image is comprised of two dimensions, a cognitive component (described as the positioning of organizations along some factual continuum) and the evaluative component (corresponding to established preferences among objects).

With respect to when or how individuals form images of organizations, several scholars suggest that image is developed over long periods of time, based on secondary sources and a more or less random accumulation of information (Behling, Labovitz, and Gainer, 1968; Gellerman, 1964). In particular, it has been suggested that images are acquired long before potential applicants begin to seek employment (Behling, et al., 1968).

Image and Attraction

Given an understanding of what image is and where it comes from, our next step is to speculate as to why it might be related to recruitment and attraction. First, image may influence applicant attraction directly. Social identity theory (Tajfel & Turner, 1985) suggests that self-concepts are shaped in part by the organizations to which we belong. When one's employer is viewed favorably (by oneself or by others), organizational membership is self-enhancing and results in positive social outcomes, such as approval. Conversely, when one's employer is viewed in a negative light, employment can lead to negative outcomes, such as depression and stress (Dutton, Dukerich, & Harquail, 1994). Therefore all else equal, potential applicants may prefer organizations with positive images.

Second, an organization's image may influence potential applicants' receptivity to recruitment messages. For example, Belt and Paolillo (1982) argued that recruitment ads must arrest attention if they are to be effective. Studies of perception have demonstrated that we often attend to what is familiar (Christie & Klein, 1995). As a result, ads placed by companies with a strong image (i.e., highly familiar companies) may draw more attention than ads placed by lesser-known companies.

Finally, and perhaps most simply, at early stages of recruitment, potential applicants may have little or no knowledge of the organization other than its image. Advertisements, postings, and other initial recruitment contacts often provide very little information, so applicants may rely on general impressions of the organization in lieu of more specific knowledge.

Our understanding of potential applicants' responses to recruitment, then, can be enhanced by studying the impact of organizational image. In particular, it would be helpful to know whether image influences individuals' behavior as they search for jobs, and by what mechanisms it does so. Also, if significant effects exist, it would be interesting to know whether and how organizational image can be manipulated for the sake of enhancing recruitment effectiveness. Though there is a small amount of empirical literature on this topic, we are a long way from fully understanding these issues.

Four studies in the existing recruitment literature examine relationships between organizational image and attraction. Tom (1971), using a sample of 100 graduating students at the University of California, asked subjects to evaluate their most and least preferred employer using a 15-scale personality assessment measure and a six-scale values assessment instrument. Subjects later described themselves using these same instruments. Tom found that applicants tended to prefer employers whose images corresponded to their own self-images.

Belt and Paolillo (1982) studied reactions of graduate and undergraduate college students to advertisements for manager jobs in fast food restaurants. In this study, image was manipulated by including firms that a pilot study had identified as having either high or low image favorability. Belt and Paolillo found that 30% of variation in whether subjects stated that they would respond to recruitment advertisements (i.e., apply for the job) could be attributed to organizational image: the more favorable the image, the more likely that subjects would apply for jobs.

Gatewood et al. (1993) examined the impact of organizational image by investigating the willingness of a group of college students to apply for jobs with companies whose image had been evaluated previously by a comparable group of students. In their study, subjects were presented with the organization's name only and were asked to indicate their probability of applying for the job. Gatewood et al. found that the probability of application (based on name only) and organizational image were highly correlated (r=.90). They found a lower correlation between probability of application and overall image when subjects also were exposed to recruitment advertisements (r=.57). In this second scenario, reactions to the advertisement (what Gatewood et al. referred to as "recruitment image") explained more variance (59.7%) in probability of application than did overall image (32.3%). Still, the amount of variation explained by overall image remained substantial.

Turban and Greening (1997) examined relationships between corporate social performance, reputation (essentially, image) and organizational attraction. They posited that corporate social performance (i.e., the firm's tendency to act responsibly in dealings with employees, customers, and the community) would predict corporate image, which in turn would be related to attraction. In their study, corporate social responsibility data for 189 firms were obtained from the Kinder, Lydenberg, Domini, and Company data base. These 189 firms were then rated as to reputation by a sample of 75 college seniors, and as to attractiveness by a sample of 34 college seniors. Their findings supported the argument that corporate social performance is related to reputation, and that reputation is related to attractiveness as an employer. It should be noted, however, that Turban and Greening eliminated from analysis firms that were unfamiliar to most (two thirds or more) of their student subjects. Therefore, we cannot determine how these students would react to unfamiliar companies.

These four studies suggest that image influences early reactions to potential employers. However, it should be noted that none of these studies assessed actual application behaviors—rather, they assessed willingness to apply or general impressions of organizational attractiveness. Furthermore, of these studies, only Tom (1971) dealt directly with the question of *why* image influences recruitment outcomes. His study was framed specifically to test a self-concept explanation for the role of image, and his data supported that hypothesis. Future image research should examine actual behaviors as well as possible reasons for those behaviors.

Perhaps more troubling are differences in the ways these studies measured image. Tom's (1971) approach was to collect very detailed impressions of the focal organizations. These fine-grained evaluations seem inconsistent with definitions of image as a general impression. Belt and Paolillo (1982), Gatewood et al. (1993), and Turban and Greening (1997) used general assessments that seem closer to the definitions of image described above. However, these studies assessed only the favorability of image, and ignored other dimensions of image, such as its strength and clarity. Thus we cannot say anything conclusive about the effect of these other dimensions on applicant reactions.

In particular, existing studies are limited by the fact that they intentionally focused on familiar companies. Belt and Paolillo (1982) used pilot testing to ensure that the companies would be known to their subjects. Gatewood et al. (1993) had subjects evaluate image only if they indicated familiarity with a company. Turban and Greening (1997) eliminated from analysis companies that were not recognized by the majority of their subjects. Thus these studies shed little light on how unfamiliar companies—in other words, companies that have no particular image—are evaluated by job seekers. However, both Gatewood et al. and Turban and Greening provide some evidence on this question. Gatewood et al. found a strong positive correlation between familiarity and image, and Turban and Greening found that unfamiliar firms had less positive reputations and were seen as less attractive as employers than were more familiar firms.

In addition, Gatewood et al.'s (1993) finding that images differ across different subject groups raises questions about whether image assessments should be aggregated. It would be inappropriate to speak of image at the organizational level if individuals hold varying images of the same organization. On the other hand, there may be identifiable subgroups of individuals who hold consistent images of particular companies, and aggregation at this level may be warranted. Clearly, the proper measurement of organizational image is an area that merits greater attention than it has so far received.

Practical Implications: Is Image Malleable?

Limitations of the existing literature notwithstanding, it does appear that image matters to potential applicants. This raises the very practical question of whether image is malleable. Can organizations whose image causes them to lose (or fail to attract) applicants modify their image? How might that be done? Questions such as these require an understanding of how organizational images are formed. Again, though we do not have a great deal of research pertaining to this question, there is some helpful evidence. Gatewood et al. (1993) examined a small set of potential determinants of image, in large part following Fombrun and Shanley's (1990) study of Fortune 500 reputations. They also addressed whether the same determinants applied for different groups of individuals (college students versus industry executives). They concluded that whereas executives base their images on hard economic performance indicators, college students tend to rely primarily on familiarity as a determinant of image. For the students, organization image was highly correlated with a variety of measures related to familiarity with, or exposure to, the organization in question: overall familiarity, knowing someone who works for the company, using its products or services, having studied the firm in class, frequency of exposure to company advertisements. Interestingly, the old adage that "there is no such thing as bad publicity" seems to hold here. Relationships between various indicators of familiarity and organizational image were consistently positive. Similarly, Turban and Greening (1997) found that familiar firms had better reputations and were viewed more favorably as employers than were unfamiliar firms.

What do these findings suggest with respect to the manipulation or malleability of organizational image? First, they suggest that image may be more malleable among some groups of applicants than others. It may be very difficult to change the images held by executives, who base their impressions on detailed knowledge of businesses in their industry. In contrast, changing image in the minds of relatively naïve college graduates may not be difficult: it may simply be a question of increasing exposure through advertising campaigns, campus visits, or other means. There is anecdotal evidence of companies taking such steps to enhance recruitment. For example, in 1990, U.S. corporations spent $1.47 billion on advertising intended not to sell a product but rather to create a favorable impression of the corporation itself (Alvarez, 1991). While the purposes of such advertising campaigns are many, one important purpose is to enhance the organization's ability to attract potential employees (Katayama, 1990; Martin, 1987). Along the same lines, burgeoning need for new accountants coupled with declining accounting enrollment rates among college students has caused accounting firms to attempt to improve their campus image by making more (and more interesting) campus visits (Yeager, 1991). However, the actual effectiveness of such campaigns has not been assessed within the recruitment literature.

In short, there seems to be an imbalance between practitioner and academic attention to the matter of image. Existing image research only begins to scratch the surface of what we ought to know, and there is much room to further our understanding of recruitment through additional research into the measurement, antecedents and consequences of organizational image. For example, we might consider more extensive sets of possible determinants of image, such as firm size, industry, location, and so on. We might also attempt to identify factors leading to unfavorable images, such as involvement in controversial lawsuits or unpopular industries. We might also further explore differences in image formation across applicant groups, which might tie in to decisions to target specific applicant populations. (For example, does an organization's image vary geographically, and if so, should organizations recruit within the region where their image is most favorable?) Application of impression formation literature (e.g., Asch, 1946; Mellers, Richards, & Birnbaum, 1992; O'Keefe & Delia, 1982) might suggest additional interesting questions, such as whether specific determinants of image play central or peripheral roles in the formation of image. With respect to the consequences of image, as noted earlier, studies focusing on behaviors rather than intentions, studies including unfamiliar organizations, and studies investigating why image influences applicants are all needed.

Reactions to Recruitment Materials

As discussed in the previous section, job seekers begin looking for jobs with some mental image of at least some of the potential employers they will consider. They are then exposed to information about potential employers through the organizations' recruitment efforts, and they use that information, perhaps along with whatever information the organization's image conveys, to make their first critical job search decision: whether or not to apply for particular jobs.

One stream of research relevant to the decision to apply investigates reactions to recruitment materials, such as advertisements or recruitment brochures. Job seekers frequently scan such materials before deciding whether to become applicants, and several studies (reviewed below) indicate that such materials do influence the decision to apply. The question of *how* these materials influence potential applicants is of substantial interest to recruitment professionals, as indicated by the frequency with which these issues are addressed in the practitioner literature (e.g., Koch, 1990; Laabs, 1991; Mamarchev, 1996; Martin, 1987; McCarthy, 1989). In contrast, there is fairly little scholarly literature on this topic.

Attracting Applicants' Attention

Effective recruitment materials must first attract the attention of potential applicants, and then persuade them to act (i.e., to apply). Much of the practitioner literature on recruitment materials focuses on attracting attention. This issue has substantial practical importance, as any single firm's recruitment materials typically must compete against a host of other advertisements on the newspaper page, brochures in the placement office, or postings at the employment agency. Indeed, the pressure of this competition for attention has caused some organizations to find other less crowded venues for reaching candidates, such as direct mail (Martin, 1987). By and large, discussions of how to attract attention focus on style rather than content. The use of novel, creative formats is often stressed in identifying award-winning recruitment campaigns or in prescribing how to design recruitment ads, as is the use of humor (e.g., Koch, 1989; Koch, 1990). In addition, the size, position (e.g., on a newspaper page), color and font used have been related to ability to attract attention (Redman & Matthews, 1992).

In contrast to the level of practitioner interest, recruitment scholars have largely ignored the question of how to attract attention to recruitment materials. There may be several reasons for the dearth of studies on this topic. First, the question has been addressed extensively in the consumer behavior literature, and there may be little reason to believe that recruitment materials are different from any other kind of consumer campaign. Perhaps it is thought that these issues are best studied by marketing experts. Second, it may be that the factors that influence attention change so rapidly that the usefulness of academic research, with its lengthy review process and publication lags, is limited (Redman & Matthews, 1992). What was novel, and therefore effective, this year may be ordinary and ineffective next year, and research conclusions as a result may become obsolete before they are even published.

The Content of Recruitment Materials

When academics do study reactions to recruitment materials, they tend to focus on content rather than style. Specifically, studies have examined general information characteristics, such as the total amount of information provided in recruitment materials and the nature of that information (i.e., its specificity, uniqueness, and variation) as well as reactions to particular job or organizational attributes described in recruitment materials.

General information characteristics. Three studies assessed relationships between the amount of information provided in recruitment materials and job seekers' willingness to apply for the position described. Barber and Roehling (1993), in a verbal protocol study of applicant reactions to job postings, provided evidence that potential applicants attend to the amount of information provided in recruitment materials. Subjects evaluating four hypothetical job postings commented on the adequacy of the information they provided without being prompted to do so, and at least some of the subjects indicated that information adequacy influenced their decision to apply. In addition, subjects evaluated the posting that provided the least information as the least attractive of the four. Barber and Roehling also found that subjects paid more attention to attributes for which specific information (e.g., exact starting salary) rather than vague information (e.g., "competitive" salaries) was provided.

Gatewood et al. (1993), as part of the image study described previously, also assessed the role played by the amount of information provided. They examined college student reactions to 13 recruitment advertisements appearing in the *College Placement Council Annual.* They content-coded the total amount of information provided in each of the advertisements, and found a strong positive correlation between amount of information provided and probability of responding to the advertisement.

Herriot and Rothwell (1981) experimentally manipulated the content of recruitment brochures, such that some contained a high number of mentions of two job attributes (opportunity to do research, variety of work) and others contained a low number of mentions. They found that brochures with high content had a positive impact on subjects' intention to apply for a job but that this effect deteriorated over time. The amount of information provided in the brochure strongly influenced application intentions measured immediately after subjects saw the brochure but had a lesser impact when application intentions were measured again one week later.

Two studies focused directly on the impact of information specificity on application decisions. Belt and Paollilo (1982), as part of the image study already discussed, examined the impact of specificity of candidate qualification requirements on likelihood of response to a hypothetical recruitment advertisement for a restaurant manager job. Based on anecdotal evidence, they anticipated that more specific ads would generate fewer, but more useful and appropriate, respondents. However, only the quantity of applicants was actually assessed. Belt and Paollilo did not find significant differences in the likelihood of responding to the ads as a function of qualification specificity.

Mason and Belt (1986) had student subjects review hypothetical job advertisements for electrical engineering positions that varied in terms of the specificity of job descriptions (characteristics of the job) and job specifications (qualifications required for the job). Based on the theory of work adjustment (Dawis, Lofquist, & Weiss, 1968), they argued that potential applicants screen for matches between their interests and abilities, on the one hand, and the requirements and rewards offered by the company, on the other. Mason and Belt anticipated that less qualified applicants would be more likely to drop out when job descriptions and job specifications were specific. They found that detailed job specifications did tend to "weed out" unqualified applicants, increasing the efficiency of the recruitment process. Evidence regarding job description specificity was somewhat mixed. Qualified applicants were most likely to respond to ads featuring specific qualifications and vague descriptions. Yet when the same subjects were asked to rank order the ads in terms of their attractiveness, they stated that they preferred the ads that were specific with respect to both qualifications and job description.

Other information characteristics that have been studied include information uniqueness and variability. Barber and Roehling (1993) found that attribute information that was unusual or extreme (e.g., unusually generous vacation packages, particularly strong EEO statements) received more attention than attributes set at more ordinary levels. And Rynes, Schwab, and Heneman (1983) found that one attribute (compensation) had greater influence on the decision to apply when there was greater variation in compensation across job alternatives.

Taken as a whole, this literature suggests that recruitment materials should be informative. They should address a range of job or organization characteristics, and they should provide specific information about those characteristics. However, there are relatively few studies examining any one of these points, and additional replication is needed before strong conclusions can be drawn.

In addition, the possibility of information overload should be considered. None of the existing studies has presented exceptionally large amounts of information, even in their "high information" conditions. Therefore, it may well be that the positive relationship between applicant reactions and information holds only up to a point: if recruitment materials contain too much information, they may overwhelm applicants and have a less positive (if not negative) effect.

Furthermore, none of the studies reviewed above dealt with actual application decisions but rather assessed willingness to apply. The fact that several of these studies (e.g., Barber & Roehling, 1993; Rynes, et al., 1983) dealt with fictitious companies adds to the hypothetical nature of this research. Though existing studies provide a good starting point for understanding the impact of amount and specificity of information on job application decisions, at this point research confirming these findings in a field context is warranted.

Specific content issues. Given that recruitment materials appear to at least have the capacity to influence application behavior, an important question is, *which* job or organization characteristics should be described? In other words, how does information content influence application decisions? Research has examined the impact of compensation, location, and diversity or fairness policies on application decisions.

Role of compensation: Practitioner reports consistently suggest that recruitment materials should include information about compensation (Laabs, 1991; Redman & Matthews, 1992). One report of managerial responses to recruitment ads found that 91% of the sample felt that it was important for ads to contain salary information, 64% indicated that the absence of salary information would reduce their likelihood of responding to the ad, and 67% stated that salary information would determine whether they would even read the entire advertisement (Price Waterhouse study, 1988; reported in Redman & Matthews, 1992).

Two academic research studies focused extensively on the role of compensation on the decision to apply. Rynes et al. (1983), using a policy-capturing design, had subjects evaluate a series of hypothetical jobs. They found that pay level (the amount of salary provided) significantly influenced decisions to apply, and that this influence was greater when subjects were exposed to salary offers that varied substantially. Cable and Judge (1994), also using policy-capturing, similarly concluded that pay policies had significant influence on the decision to actively pursue a job. They found that this influence was not limited to pay level but included other aspects of pay, such as whether pay was based on individual or group performance and the amount of pay that was variable (or "at risk"). In addition, they found that the impact of pay policies was moderated by individual difference characteristics. For example, more materialistic job seekers were more strongly influenced by pay level than were less materialistic subjects.

The importance of pay in application decisions is supported by two other studies that focused less directly on compensation issues. Barber and Roehling (1993), in the verbal protocol study described above, found that salary and benefits ranked second and third, respectively, among 10 attributes in the amount of attention they received from potential applicants. Schwoerer and Rosen (1989) found that salary level was positively related to the decision to apply. However, in a study focusing on family-friendly human resource policies (discussed in more detail below), Honeycutt and Rosen (1997) failed to find a significant relationship between salary level and attraction to an organization.

Williams and Dreher (1992) also examined the relationship between compensation and applicant behavior, although their perspective was that of the organization and not the individual applicant. Using a sample of 352 U.S. banks, they examined the relationships between compensation system attributes (pay level and the level and flexibility of benefits) and recruitment outcomes, including size of applicant pool, acceptance rates, and length of time required to fill positions. The first outcome, size of applicant pool, is the dependent measure most closely related to the decision to apply. Williams and Dreher (1992) did *not* find a significant relationship between pay level and number of applicants. However, some aspects of benefits programs were associated with applicant pool size: Banks that devoted a large percentage of total compensation dollars attracted larger numbers of applicants, whereas banks that offered flexible benefits attracted smaller numbers of applicants.

Geographic location: The Price Waterhouse study of managerial responses to recruitment advertisements (cited in Redman & Matthews, 1992) found that 84% of respondents felt that location was a key determinant of whether they would apply for a job. Though I found no recruitment studies that focused extensively on the role of location, several studies support its importance in initial application decisions. Both Rynes and Lawler (1983) and Barber and Roehling (1993) found location to be a particularly important element in the decision to apply. In fact, Barber and Roehling indicated that in many cases location was cited as the primary reason for deciding not to apply. We know little about individual difference factors that might influence the importance of location in the context of recruitment. However, there is a rich literature on employee attitudes toward transfers involving relocation that may well generalize to this context. This research has found, for example, that employees with family obligations (e.g., children and spouses, especially working spouses) and strong community ties (e.g., long tenure in the community) are less likely to accept relocation opportunities, and that individuals in early career stages are more likely to relocate (Noe, Steffy, & Barber, 1988). These factors might suggest that location is a less serious issue in college recruitment, where potential applicants are younger and less likely to have family obligations and community ties, and a more serious issue in the recruitment of experienced employees.

Diversity-related studies: Issues related to the management of demographically diverse employees have been at the forefront of both business and society at large during the 1990s. Not surprisingly, then, several studies have explored the impact of diversity-related policies on application decisions. Barber and Roehling (1993) found that potential applicants responded more strongly to an equal employment opportunity (EEO) statement encouraging women and minorities to apply than to a statement merely indicating that the organization was an equal opportunity employer. Female subjects tended to have favorable reactions to the stronger statement, whereas male subjects tended to have negative reactions. However, due to the nature of Barber and Roehling's design, these reactions cannot be tied directly to the decision to apply.

Saks, Leck, and Saunders (1995) examined the impact of equitable hiring practices in the context of the application form itself. Selection practices can influence potential employees' view of the organization, and therefore their willingness to pursue jobs with that organization, as discussed in more detail in the next chapter. Application blanks, which are often the first step in the selection process, have the potential to attract or turn off potential employees very early in the recruitment phase. Those who are offended by application blanks may simply fail to fill them out and return them to the organization. Saks et al. (1995), in the only study I found that explicitly examined this issue, had college student subjects review simulated application blanks for a hypothetical company. Two aspects of the applications were manipulated: whether the application form included discriminatory questions (e.g., questions about gender, marital status, and age), and whether the form stated that the firm had an equal opportunity policy. Saks et al. found that applicants were less motivated to pursue jobs when application blanks contained discriminatory items and the organization was not believed to have an EEO policy.

Williams and Bauer (1994) went beyond EEO/affirmative action concerns to examine the effects of diversity policies on organizational attractiveness. Policies aimed at effective diversity management are intended to enable all employees to perform to their highest potential, a much broader goal than merely ceasing to discriminate (EEO) or ensuring that women and minorities are hired. In their study, Williams and Bauer (1994) created two recruitment brochures presenting a fictitious company. The brochures were identical except in one respect: One brochure identified the company as having a diversity management policy; the other had no such statement. (Both, however, indicated that the company was an affirmative action employer.) Four hundred forty-eight upper level college students were randomly assigned to one or the other condition. Results indicated that the firm was seen as more attractive when it was portrayed as having a diversity policy.

Honeycutt and Rosen (1997) examined the impact of family-friendly human resource policies on organizational attraction. They asked 263 Executive MBA students and MBA alumni to evaluate an announcement regarding a job with a fictitious company. Descriptions of career paths were manipulated across subjects, such that some read a statement indicating that only traditional (career-primary) career paths were available, while others read statements indicating that dual paths (career-primary or career-and-family as distinct alternatives) or flexible paths (all employees have the flexibility to balance work and nonwork) were available. Honeycutt and Rosen (1997) found that flexible career paths were associated with greater attraction to the organization for all participants, although this effect was strongest among individuals for whom the family role was particularly salient.

In summary, there is evidence that salary, location, and diversity policies *can* influence application decisions. However, our understanding of which attributes actually *do* influence application decisions is somewhat limited. First, investigations of this topic tend to focus on a narrow range of attributes, both within and across studies. While the tendency to focus on compensation, diversity/fairness, and to a lesser extent location is to some extent justified by descriptive data, it is not clear why other attributes (for example, job duties and responsibilities) have been ignored. In addition, our knowledge of the combined effect of these elements is limited by the fact that most studies focus on only a few attributes. Furthermore, all of the studies reviewed above dealt with intended rather than actual applications and used fictitious rather than actual companies. Again, there is a need for confirmation of these findings in field settings.

Application Decision Processes

The research described immediately above deals with individual reactions to the style and content of recruitment materials. A second but equally important question is *how* individuals decide whether to apply for jobs. By what processes are reactions to recruitment materials, as well as other reactions to the company, combined to result in application decisions?

One fundamental issue that has not been addressed directly is whether and when there is enough variation in application decisions to make further investigation into this process worthwhile. It is possible that job application decisions have received less attention than later job choice decisions because job application decisions are not mutually exclusive. The decision to apply to one company in no way prevents job seekers from applying to other companies. The number of applications filed is limited only by the amount of resources required to apply, which may be quite small. One might argue, then, that job seekers do not have to make a choice at this stage of the process— there would be little reason *not* to apply for any and all jobs encountered.

Though it is certainly true that job seekers need not choose a single organization at this stage, it seems unlikely that they have the time and energy to apply for all possible opportunities. As a result, decisions made at the initial application stage should be characterized as *screening* decisions that reduce the set of potential opportunities, rather than as *choices* favoring one opportunity over all others. Research reviewed above suggests that significant screening might occur, as none of the studies appeared to suffer lack of variation in the application decision variable. For example, Barber and Roehling (1993) found that subjects declined to apply for 30% of the jobs they reviewed, despite the fact that jobs were not plentiful during the time period covered by the study. Of course, these findings are merely suggestive, as they involved hypothetical job scenarios. The fact is that we know little about how much screening occurs at this stage, or under what circumstances potential applicants are more or less likely to exclude a large proportion of potential opportunities. Research along these lines would add significantly to our understanding of the context in which application decisions are made.

On the reasonable presumption that some screening does occur, two process issues regarding the decision to apply have been studied: whether expectancy theory adequately captures the decision to apply, and whether job seekers use compensatory or noncompensatory decision strategies in deciding to apply for jobs.

Expectancy theory (Vroom, 1964) is one of the most widely studied and accepted models of decision making, and therefore it is no surprise that various authors have studied its usefulness in explaining job application decisions. Expectancy theory portrays motivation to exert effort toward some particular end as a multiplicative function of two factors: the individual's perception that he or she can obtain a particular outcome (referred to as *expectancy,* or *E*) and the individual's assessment of the attractiveness of that outcome, a combination of the likelihood that the outcome has certain characteristics (called its *instrumentality,* or *I*) and the attractiveness of those characteristics (their *valence,* or *V*). Mathematically, the model can be depicted as:

(2.1) $\text{Exertion of effort} = f[E \times \Sigma(V^*I)].$

In the context of application decisions, expectancy refers to the potential applicant's beliefs that he or she would be successful in obtaining employment with the organization. The attractiveness of that employment would be a function of the attributes the job was expected to possess as well as the attractiveness of those attributes to the potential applicant.

Studies of expectancy theory's ability to predict job application decisions are limited in number, and they tend to focus on individual elements of the model rather than the model in totality. For example, Herriott and Rothwell (1981), in a study using recruitment brochures for hypothetical companies, examined the instrumentality component of the model. They found that, although brochures did influence the decision to apply, there was no evidence that they did so through their impact on instrumentalities. Therefore their study failed to provide support for the expectancy model. Rynes and Lawler (1983) examined the expectancy component of the model rather than the instrumentality component. They manipulated information about the subjects' probability of receiving an offer in a within-subject policy-capturing design. Their results were at best partially supportive of the expectancy model, as there was substantial individual difference in the degree to which expectancy perceptions influenced the decision to apply. Finally, Barber and Roehling (1993) found that beliefs regarding the probability of hire had little influence on the decision to apply in a context in which expectancy information was not directly provided but rather had to be inferred by applicants. Overall, what little evidence we have regarding the usefulness of expectancy theory in explaining job application decisions is discouraging.

A second stream of decision-process research sheds additional light on the relevance of expectancy theory in explaining application decisions. This stream focuses on whether job seekers use compensatory or noncompensatory decision-making models. The expectancy model is inherently compensatory: Because it is multiplicative in nature, high "scores" on one dimension can offset low "scores" on another. Alternatively, noncompensatory models suggest that job seekers set minimum standards for specific job or organization characteristics, and reject all opportunities that fall below those standards, regardless of what else they may have to offer.

Three studies addressed the question of whether compensatory or noncompensatory models are used in determining whether to apply for jobs, and all support the noncompensatory view. Rynes, Schwab, and Heneman (1983) explicitly tested whether the application decision was compensatory versus noncompensatory. Focusing on salary levels, they found that most subjects rejected all job opportunities in which pay fell below a certain level, suggesting a noncompensatory framework. Rynes and Lawler (1983) did not explicitly test for compensatory versus noncompensatory decision making. Their results, however, suggested that at least for some subjects, both location and type of job represented noncompensatory elements (in each case, 4 of 10 subjects rejected all interviews involving a particular location or a particular type of school). Finally, Barber and Roehling (1993) found that certain job characteristics (location in particular) were used as noncompensatory screening variables. Jobs were rejected if they failed to meet requirements on this factor, regardless of other job characteristics.

Other studies, however, have reached conclusions consistent with compensatory models. For example, Schwoerer & Rosen (1989) found that high compensation levels offset the negative impact of employment-at-will statements. And Saks et al. (1995) found that having an explicit EEO policy offset the negative effect of discriminatory application blank questions. These findings may imply that potential applicants use selected job or organization characteristics as noncompensatory screening variables and allow for trade-offs among other characteristics. Investigation of which attributes are most likely to be evaluated against an absolute standard (i.e., in noncompensatory fashion) and which are most likely to be evaluated in a compensatory manner could greatly increase our understanding of this decision process. Such investigation could also inform decisions regarding the content of recruitment materials by suggesting what kind of information most essential to job seekers.

Spillover in Early Recruitment

This chapter focused primarily on two players: the organization seeking employees and the individual seeking job opportunities. This focus is consistent with the emphasis of existing research. As noted in Chapter 1, however, though these are the primary players in recruitment, they are not the only parties involved in, or influenced by, the process. Recruitment efforts associated with this first stage likely have spillover effects because they are targeted at a wide audience. They may have indirect and unintended effects on organizational outcomes through their impact on individuals who were not part of the relevant applicant population to begin with.

Such effects seem particularly likely if organizations attempt to manipulate their images in order to more successfully attract applicants. The manipulation of image would require communication that is broadly disseminated (e.g., via television, radio, or general interest publications rather than in help-wanted sections) and that changes general impressions of the organization (rather than focusing narrowly on what the organization would be like as an employer). Such communications, called image advertising, are likely to be seen and responded to by potential customers and potential investors, and may alter their behaviors toward the organization (Fombrun & Shanley, 1990). For that matter, even advertisements intended specifically to recruit (rather than to convey image) can impact other organizational constituents. For example, military recruitment campaigns, such as the U.S. Army's "Be All You Can Be" campaign may result in more political support for the armed services if they alter voter impressions of the military.

To date, recruitment research has not examined the impact of early recruitment activities on outcomes unrelated to recruitment. The reason for this may seem obvious: such effects are outside the domain of recruitment. However, increasing interest in the "bottom line" impact of human resource policies (see Chapter 5) suggests that such reasoning is too narrow, and that a complete understanding of how recruitment policies affect organizational outcomes requires examination of potential spillover effects.

Conclusion

As this chapter's title indicates, the purpose of this first stage of recruitment is to generate applicants: to convert an applicant population into an applicant pool (ideally, one with an appropriate quantity of qualified applicants). Therefore, one way to evaluate existing research related to this phase is to ask, "What do we know about how applicant pools are formed?" We know fairly little about the impact of targeting on applicant pools. We know a few things about how recruitment sources influence applicant characteristics, but the focus of source research has been on post-hire outcomes rather than on effects on applicant pools *per se*. We know that image is related to attraction to an organization, and that it therefore *ought to be* related to applicant pool size, although this effect has not been directly examined. We know that recruitment advertisements and other materials are related to applicant attraction, and again, therefore *ought to be* related to applicant pool size and composition.

In fact, however, recruitment researchers have rarely studied applicant pool characteristics as a dependent variable (see Williams & Dreher, 1992, for an exception). This is unfortunate, as applicant pool characteristics have clear implications for the efficiency of recruitment and the effectiveness of selection. Additional studies focusing on the nature of applicant pools might shed considerable light on how recruitment really works. Such research will require a shift in research design, from the individual-level focus typical of most existing research to cross-organizational designs. Such a shift will pose methodological difficulties. Controlling for relevant differences across organizations is a challenging task, as is obtaining high response rates to organizational surveys. Nonetheless, such research is needed to advance our understanding of this first stage of recruitment.[1]

Researchers interested in contributing to our knowledge of early recruitment outcomes also need to consider *potential* applicants who decide *not* to apply. Those who ignored an advertisement or failed to respond to a search firm's call are "missing persons" in recruitment research, although their decisions are surely important to organizations. Turban, Eyring and Campion (1993) demonstrated that at later stages of recruitment, the factors that cause a job offer to be rejected are different from the factors that cause a job offer to be accepted. A similar phenomenon may occur with respect to the decision to become an applicant, but we cannot know whether that is the case until non-applicants become part of our research domain.

Inclusion of non-applicants will also require different research methodologies from those traditionally employed. In this instance, the problem is one of sampling. Applicants are easily identified through organizational records or through placement office data. Non-applicants are substantially harder to find, particularly if one is interested in non-college populations. Here, we might rely on techniques used by other disciplines (such as marketing) to identify appropriate subjects. For example, telephone surveys could be used to identify whether individuals who are part of the targeted applicant population reside at a particular address; mail surveys assessing why those individuals either did or did not apply could then be sent.

In short, many interesting questions about initial recruitment activities remain unaddressed by empirical research. Though the data required to address those questions will not be easily obtained, opportunities to contribute substantially to the literature are great. And, because initial recruitment outcomes are the foundation on which later recruitment successes must be built, the practical implications of research focusing on this stage are also substantial.

NOTE

1. This research approach is discussed in more detail in Chapter 5.

3 Maintaining Applicant Status

This chapter covers the second phase of recruitment, during which specific individuals (applicants) are recruited by the organization. The organization's goals during this phase are to maintain applicants' interest so that they will continue to pursue employment (typically, by undergoing a variety of selection and screening procedures) and will accept job offers in the event that they are extended. Applicants focus on narrowing down their initial pool of potential employers and acquiring enough information to be able to make a choice regarding whether or not to accept a position if one is offered. This stage of recruitment is characterized by significant interpersonal contact—specific organizational agents (recruiters and others involved in the hiring process) interact with specific applicants. These interactions may be quite time consuming, particularly as applicants proceed through the recruitment and selection process; and the information obtained by both parties during this phase is substantially more detailed than what might be acquired during the previous phase. In other words, this phase involves intensive, as opposed to extensive, search.

Like the first phase, this phase encompasses a variety of recruitment activities, from initial face-to-face contacts with applicants (through job fairs, placement office interviews, or other initial screening interviews) to "site visits" (extended interviews on company premises that often run one or more full days). In addition, it is during this phase that the organization engages in selection activities, such as psychological or physical testing, drug testing, or testing in assessment centers. Though these activities are not part of the domain of recruitment per se, they can influence applicant impressions of the organization, as discussed below. Despite the variety of activities that occur during this phase, much of the existing research focuses on the initial screening interview. Relatively few studies have investigated other types of initial contacts or the more extended interactions that occur later in the process. Therefore, this chapter describes research that does exist with respect to the initial interview and speculates about research that ought to exist regarding other aspects of this phase. Again, material is organized chronologically. Initial screening interviews are discussed first, and both applicant and recruiter perspectives are considered. Later activities—site visits, administrative processes, and selection procedures—are then discussed. Finally, research on communication realism is introduced.

The material on realism represents a partial exception to the chronological format of the chapter. As Wanous and Colella (1989) noted, realistic information can be provided at almost any point during recruitment, and sometimes is provided after applicants have become employees. As a result, this material could have been placed at any point in this chapter (or, for that matter, in earlier or later chapters). My decision to place the material at the end of this chapter is, admittedly, somewhat arbitrary.

Initial Face-to-Face Contacts

Initial contacts between organizational representatives and applicants are potentially quite important from an attraction standpoint, as first impressions of an organization's employees can lead to the formation of opinions that are relatively hard to dislodge later (Tversky & Kahneman, 1974). The importance of first impressions has been studied extensively with respect to selection: Recruiters have been found to judge applicants fairly quickly. Applicants may be less quick to judge organizations, as they generally have a smaller choice set and less pressure to quickly reduce that set. Nonetheless, impressions formed during initial personal contacts may critically influence later reactions and behaviors.

Initial contacts between applicant and organization can take many forms. Initial screening interviews, whether on college campuses, on the employer's premises, or elsewhere, are one of the most common means of establishing interpersonal contact, but there are others. In particular, organizations facing shortages of employees in specific areas have turned to more casual contacts, such as open houses and job fairs as means of interacting with potential employees (Glickstein & Ramer, 1988).

Research on the effects of these initial contacts is severely skewed in favor of the screening interview in general, and the campus interview in particular. Following a review of this research, I will discuss how other forms of initial contact differ from the placement interview and suggest needed research along these lines.

Initial Screening Interviews

This section focuses on the most commonly researched aspect of face-to-face recruitment, the initial interview. These interviews are generally brief in duration (typically lasting about 30 minutes). During that time, recruiters attempt to acquire information about the applicant and also to provide information about the organization. Similarly, and simultaneously, applicants attempt to provide information about their own qualifications and at the same time acquire information about the organization. The interview, then, is a dynamic exchange between two parties, and there are many opportunities for one party to shape the attitudes and behaviors of the other. Thus one might argue that the interview is best studied as an interactive event (Taylor & Giannantonio, 1993). However, as Graves (1993) argued, we are likely to generate more interesting and relevant hypotheses about interactions between recruiters and applicants if we have a clear understanding of the perspective of each of the parties taken separately. Toward that end, I review research focusing on either the applicant perspective or the recruiter perspective before discussing interactive models.

Applicant-Centered Research

Research on applicant reactions to screening interviews has a fairly long history. A significant body of work investigates applicant reactions to recruiters (i.e., individuals conducting the initial interview), specifically, to their traits, behaviors, and demographic characteristics. In addition, there are a number of studies focusing on reactions to the interview process as well as to the type of information conveyed during the interview. This section reviews that research.

Reactions to recruiter traits and behaviors. A reasonably large number of studies have examined applicant reactions to recruiter traits (personality characteristics) and behaviors. Because applicants infer recruiter traits from their behaviors, the two are difficult to disentangle, and therefore will be considered jointly. Whereas the earliest work on applicant reactions to recruiter traits and behaviors is primarily descriptive, more recent studies offer (and in some cases test) a theoretical rationale for these effects. Signaling theory (Spence, 1973, 1974) suggests that decision makers faced with uncertainty and incomplete information use what information they do have as the basis for inferences about missing information. Because job applicants often have limited information about jobs and organizations, they may use recruiter traits and behaviors as signals of important aspects of the employment opportunity. More specifically, as articulated by Rynes (1991), recruiters may serve as the basis for two types of applicant inferences: inferences regarding the applicant's probability of receiving a job offer, and inferences regarding job or organizational characteristics.

Among the earliest studies of applicant reactions to recruiters are Alderfer and McCord (1970) and Schmitt and Coyle (1976). Alderfer and McCord (1970), in a field survey of graduating MBA students, found that supportive and competent recruiter behaviors were positively associated with applicant expectations regarding whether they would receive an offer as well as applicants' reported probability of accepting that offer. Schmitt and Coyle, in a survey of graduating college seniors, assessed applicant perceptions of 58 personality or behavioral characteristics, which were reduced to six general factors. A variety of dependent variables were explored, including perceived likelihood of receiving an offer, overall attractiveness of the company, and likelihood of accepting an offer. Applicants' perceptions regarding their likelihood of receiving a job offer were related to interviewer warmth, whether the interviewer exhibited a businesslike manner, and the amount of information provided by the recruiter. Both overall company attractiveness and likelihood of accepting a job offer were predicted by recruiter warmth and businesslike manner. Recruiter warmth had the most consistent impact across the set of 9 dependent variables assessed; the amount of information provided by the recruiter was positively related to 7 dependent variables.

Rynes and Miller (1983) used an experimental design to assess relationships between recruiter characteristics and attraction to jobs. In two separate studies using videotaped mock interviews, Rynes and Miller manipulated recruiter warmth (both studies) and the amount of information provided by the recruiter (Study 1 only). After viewing the videotapes, college student subjects were asked to put themselves in the role of the applicant and evaluate the recruiter, the job itself, whether the organization would pursue the applicant/ subject for employment, and whether the applicant/subject would continue to pursue the job following the interview by accepting a second interview invitation or by accepting a job if one were offered. In Study 1, recruiter warmth was significantly and positively related to evaluations of the recruiter, hiring expectancies, and willingness to accept an invitation for a second interview but unrelated to assessments of job attractiveness or willingness to accept a job offer. The amount of information provided was positively and significantly related to evaluation of the recruiter, hire expectancies, job attractiveness, and willingness to make follow-up phone calls after the interview. In Study 2, recruiter warmth was once again significantly associated with evaluations of the recruiters themselves and of hire expectancies. However, in this study, which also manipulated job characteristics, recruiter warmth had no impact on job attractiveness or on willingness to pursue the job.

Powell (1984) surveyed college seniors regarding reactions to a job for which they had just interviewed. He assessed two recruiter characteristics: warmth (or affect) and recruiter knowledge (more specifically, the amount of information provided by the recruiter). Like Rynes and Miller's (1983) second study, Powell also incorporated information on job characteristics in his model. He found that recruiter factors were not significantly related to likelihood of job acceptance when assessed alongside job attribute information. However, in a follow- up study based on the same data set, Powell (1991) also entered pre- interview impressions of the job into his model and concluded that recruiter characteristics were significantly associated with applicant reactions when both pre- and post-interview beliefs about job characteristics were controlled. Specifically, recruiter warmth was positively related to applicant expectations regarding the probability of receiving an offer and likelihood of accepting an offer. The magnitude of the latter relationship, however, was not large.

Liden and Parsons (1986), in the sole study of this stream to use noncollege subjects, used post-interview questionnaires to investigate relationships between perceptions of the interviewer and attraction to the job among a group of applicants for seasonal, unskilled jobs. They found that applicant impressions of recruiter competence, personableness (essentially, warmth), and informativeness were positively related to evaluations of the interview and of the job, but did not find that these affective reactions influenced intentions of accepting the job offer.

Taylor and Bergmann (1987) also investigated the influence of recruiter characteristics on applicant reactions, using a longitudinal survey design and college applicants to a specific organization. With respect to the initial campus interview, they found that recruiter empathy (warmth) was significantly and positively related both to assessments of company attractiveness and to probability of offer acceptance.

Harris and Fink (1987), in a field study of college graduates using a pre- and post-interview survey design, drew 33 items assessing recruiter personality and behavior from the longer initial list used by Schmitt and Coyle. These items were reduced to four factors: personableness, competence, informativeness, and aggressiveness. Harris and Fink (1987) found that recruiter characteristics were significantly related to regard for the company and the job; specifically, competence and informativeness were positively related to regard for the company; personableness was positively related to regard for the job. In addition, aggressiveness was negatively related to regard for the job. Personableness was also significantly related to likelihood of joining the company and to expectations of receiving an offer.

Turban and Dougherty (1992), in a field study conducted in a college placement setting, assessed applicant perceptions of 22 items describing recruiter characteristics and behaviors, which were reduced to five factors, three of which are relevant to this section (the remainder are addressed in following sections): recruiter interest in the applicant, recruiter informativeness, and recruiter intimidation of the applicant. They found that applicant expectations of the probability of receiving a job offer were positively associated with demonstration of interest in the candidate and negatively associated with intimidation. In addition, the overall attractiveness of the organization was associated with interest in the candidate and the amount of information provided by the recruiter.

Maurer, Howe, and Lee (1992), using a mail survey of a national sample of graduating engineers, examined four recruiter characteristics: recruiter performance (a composite that included degree of interest in the candidate, enthusiasm, etc.) and three separate measures of informativeness (with respect to compensation/benefits, job/career information, and security/success). They found that all four recruiter behaviors measures were positively associated with both overall response to the interview process and likelihood of offer acceptance.

Goltz and Giannantonio (1995) used an experimental approach to investigating reactions to recruiter affect. Using videotaped mock interviews and college student subjects, they manipulated recruiter "friendliness" warmth and found that friendliness was significantly and positively associated with assessments of the organization's attractiveness.

Signaling as an explanation for effects. The studies reviewed above indicate that recruiter characteristics (in particular, warmth, competence, and informativeness) are related to overall impressions of the organization and to intentions of pursuing employment with the company. As noted earlier, the primary mechanism through which recruiter traits and behaviors are expected to influence applicant reactions to the interview is signaling. It has been hypothesized that applicants make inferences about the attractiveness of the job or their probability of receiving a job offer based on recruiter characteristics, and that these inferences are directly related to applicants' decisions to pursue employment opportunities. Several studies shed light on the validity of this hypothesis.

First, six studies found evidence that recruiter traits and behaviors (most typically, warmth) are associated with job offer expectancies. These findings certainly suggest that signaling is occurring with respect to probability of hire, but they must be interpreted with caution. Most of these findings come from relatively uncontrolled survey research, in which alternative explanations for the observed associations cannot be ruled out. For example, if recruiters who actually *told* applicants that their probability of hire was good were perceived as more friendly *because* they made such statements, an association between warmth and probability of hire would be observed, but it would not be the result of signaling. In both studies by Rynes and Miller (1983), however, the content of recruiter remarks was experimentally controlled, providing stronger support for the conclusion that recruiter behaviors serve as signals regarding probability of hire.

Evidence regarding inferences about job or organizational characteristics is relatively scarce. Rynes and Miller (1983), in the first of their two experimental studies, found evidence that recruiter affect and informativeness were both associated with beliefs that the company treats its employees well. Informativeness was also associated with beliefs that the company rewards its employees well. Because the information offered by the "more informative" recruiters was carefully designed to be neutral in favorability, these findings can be attributed to signaling effects. The recruiter affect association with perceptions of how well the company treats its employees was not, however, replicated in their second study. In another tightly controlled experimental study, Goltz and Giannantonio (1995) demonstrated that recruiter friendliness was associated with a set of beliefs about the organization (e.g., whether it was prestigious, people-oriented, fair, secure). Given their design, using videotapes identical but for recruiter friendliness, these differences can be attributed to recruiter signaling.

In addition to these experimental studies, Harris and Fink (1987), in a field survey using a pre- and post-interview design, found that recruiter characteristics were related to perceptions of four organizational characteristics: the job itself, compensation/job security, work/company environment, and minor fringe benefits. Unfortunately, although this study controls for pre-interview assessments of those attributes, it does not control for whether the recruiters actually provided information about these attributes during the interview. For example, recruiter informativeness was positively associated with impressions of job attributes, which may merely suggest that these recruiters provided positive information about the attributes. Information that is actually provided, of course, need not be inferred from recruiter characteristics.

Finally, Rynes, Bretz, and Gerhart (1991), using in-depth interviews of 41 job-seeking college students, found substantial qualitative evidence of signaling, with a number of subjects indicating that they accorded influence to the recruiter because they perceived that person as representative of the company as a whole. The effect, however, was not universal. Subjects who stated they were not influenced by the recruiter tended to argue that recruiters were *not* representative of the organization. In addition, signaling effects appeared to be less likely when recruiters were not from the applicant's functional area.

Only one study failed to find any evidence supportive of signaling. Herriot and Rothwell (1981), using a pre- and post-interview field study design, found no evidence that interviews influenced applicant beliefs about favorable or unfavorable outcomes associated with employment opportunities. These authors, however, did not examine relationships between perceptions of jobs and the specific recruiter attributes (e.g., warmth) identified as signals in other research.

Although the bulk of research into the processes by which recruiter behaviors influence applicants focuses on the fairly subtle signaling mechanism, it is also possible that recruiter behaviors influence applicants via other means. For example, recruiters may behave in ways that directly influence applicant impressions. To my knowledge, only one study examines these more direct, perhaps intentional, effects. Stevens, Mitchell, and Tripp (1990) examined reactions to recruiters from a persuasion standpoint rather than a signaling standpoint. They used recruitment videotapes to manipulate the type of impression management behavior (opinion conformer, self-enhancer, other-enhancer) engaged in by recruiters and asked subjects viewing the tapes to evaluate the recruiters and also to make choices regarding which organization (in this case, university) they would prefer to join. Stevens et al. (1990) concluded that recruiters who used the opinion conformer approach were both well liked and effective in persuading applicants to join their organization. This study makes a particularly important contribution by focusing our attention on behaviors whose role in influence and persuasion is supported by existing theory and empirical research. Further research of this sort has a high probability of advancing our understanding of effective recruiter behaviors.

Reactions to Recruiters' Demographic Characteristics. Recruiters' demographic characteristics (e.g., gender, race, age, organizational level) may influence applicant reactions to organization for one of three reasons. First, the nature of the person sent to recruit can send signals about the organization or about the importance of the job for which the applicant is interviewing. For example, applicants might make inferences about organizational diversity or the organization's commitment to equal opportunity on the basis of the characteristics (gender and race in particular) of the recruiter. Or, applicants might make inferences about the status of the job for which they are interviewing on the basis of the functional area or hierarchical level of the individual sent to recruit. Alternatively, Rynes (1991) suggested that applicants may respond to recruiter demographic characteristics simply because they share the same general biases held by much of society. Finally, Maurer et al. (1992) have offered the "similarity" hypothesis. Drawing from the marketing literature, they argued that applicants respond more favorably to influence sources (e.g., recruiters) who are similar to themselves. Several studies have addressed the impact of recruiter demographic characteristics on applicant reactions, with mixed results.

Liden and Parsons (1986), in the study of entry-level job applicants described previously, found that female recruiters were perceived as more personable and informative than male recruiters. Recruiter gender was unrelated to general reactions to the interview or intentions to accept the job but was significantly related to general evaluation of the job. Despite the positive qualities attributed to female recruiters, applicants who were interviewed by female recruiters had less favorable affective reactions to the job.

Taylor and Bergmann (1987), in the longitudinal study described above, examined the impact of recruiter age, gender, race, recruiting experience, job tenure, education level, interview training, and job type on applicant perceptions of company attractiveness and their stated probability of accepting a job offer. Taylor and Bergmann found significant effects for the set of demographic variables, which accounted for 16% of the variance in company attractiveness and 15% of the variance in probability of acceptance. Company attractiveness varied as a function of recruiter age, gender, and job type (whether human resources or line management), with older, female, and HR recruiters associated with lower attraction. Probability of accepting a job offer was related to education level, with more educated recruiters associated with greater likelihood of accepting. In addition, probability of accepting an offer was related to recruiter gender, but only among female applicants. Male applicants were indifferent to recruiter gender, but female applicants reported higher probability of offer acceptance when their recruiter was male.

Turban and Dougherty (1992) assessed the relationships of recruiter gender, age, education level, and job function with applicants' expectations of receiving an offer and applicant assessments of organizational attractiveness. They found only one marginally significant main effect: Recruiter education level was negatively related to expectations of receiving an offer. They then assessed the impact of applicant and recruiter similarity with respect to gender and college attended, and found some evidence of similarity effects. Gender similarity appeared to have a positive effect on attraction for male applicants, but no effect for female applicants. Gender similarity was unrelated to expectations of receiving an offer. Similarity of educational institutions was unrelated to attraction and (surprisingly) negatively related to expectations of receiving an offer.

Maurer et al. (1992) assessed the impact of applicant/recruiter similarity with respect to age, gender, and educational background on reactions to the recruitment process and intentions to accept jobs if offered. They found that certain aspects of applicant/recruiter trait similarity were related to general reactions to the recruitment process. No age effects were observed, but applicants had more positive reactions to recruitment when the recruiter and the applicant were from the same field of study. In addition, a significant gender similarity effect was observed, but it was opposite to what was expected. General reactions to the recruitment process among females were more positive when recruiters were male (i.e., dissimilar). Maurer et al. (1992) found no relationship between demographic similarities and job acceptance.

In general, then, support for the argument that recruiter demographics influence applicant reactions is fairly weak. There is some evidence that recruiter demographics influence overall evaluations of organizations or jobs, but effects are not often replicated across studies. Further, there is little evidence that recruiter demographics influence intentions to pursue jobs. Finally, there is limited evidence of similarity effects, and what evidence exists does not often match the anticipated pattern—similarity does not necessarily lead to more favorable applicant attitudes. These weak findings may be attributed in part to the way studies of demographic effects have been designed. Most of the studies reviewed above include few demographic characteristics, with little attempt to justify why particular characteristics were chosen and why others were ignored. Only one study (Taylor & Bergmann, 1987) included a fairly broad array of demographic characteristics; this study was the only one to find significant relationships between recruiter demographic characteristics and intentions to accept the job. Furthermore, existing studies have considered specific demographic characteristics in isolation, and potentially interesting trade-offs or synergies across characteristics are ignored. Finally, there have been very few attempts to directly test the processes by which recruiter characteristics might influence applicant reactions (e.g., signaling, bias). Although current findings are not terribly promising, it may be that more comprehensive assessments of the impact of recruiter demographics would reveal stronger effects.

Reactions to the interview process. Initial interviews can be differentiated on a number of dimensions, beyond the characteristics of the recruiters involved. In this section, I discuss applicant reactions to the interview process, that is, the way the interview is conducted. Three issues are addressed: interview focus, interview structure, and interview content.

Interview focus. One aspect of the interview process that has recently been investigated is the interview's focus. Rynes (1989) clearly differentiated between two purposes of the initial interview: recruitment and selection. She noted that the balance between these two purposes (referred to as "interview focus") is variable. In some cases (most likely, where labor shortages are severe), recruiters might devote the majority of their time to persuading applicants as to the attractiveness of the organization. In other cases (in which the number of applicants perhaps far exceeds the number of jobs available), recruiters may devote more energy to screening out less desirable applicants. Thus, one interesting aspect of the interview process is the degree to which the recruiter emphasizes recruitment or selection. One might anticipate that applicants would respond more favorably to organizations when interviews focus heavily on recruitment, both because recruiters have exerted more effort toward creating those favorable impressions and because applicants who are heavily recruited may believe that their chances of receiving a job offer are particularly good. Interestingly, research on applicant reactions to interview focus does not clearly support that logic.

Several studies have assessed applicant responses to interview focus. Taylor and Bergmann (1987), in a field study of applicants recruited by a specific company, assessed how much time recruiters typically spent evaluating the applicant and how much time was typically spent "selling" the organization. They concluded that neither variable influenced applicants' perceptions of company attractiveness or their expressed probability of offer acceptance.

Macan and Dipboye (1990), in a field study conducted in a campus placement center, found weak effects for interview focus. Applicants' intentions to accept jobs were influenced by the duration of interview, the percentage of time spent gathering information, and the percentage of time spent recruiting. Taken as a set, the three variables accounted for 9% of the variance. None of the individual variables, however, was significantly related to acceptance intentions.

Turban and Dougherty (1992) also examined the role of interview focus in a college placement setting. They found that interviews emphasizing recruitment were viewed more favorably by applicants, and that interview focus explained a significant portion of the variance in job attractiveness. Ironically, when recruiters spent more time "selling" jobs, applicants perceived the jobs as less attractive. Time spent selling the company did not significantly influence applicant attraction, and no relationship between interview focus and perceived likelihood of receiving a job offer was observed.

Barber, Hollenbeck, Tower, and Phillips (1994) conducted a field experiment in which applicants for a part-time job were randomly assigned to one of two interview conditions: an interview that focused exclusively on recruitment or an interview that combined recruitment and selection. Applicants assigned to the recruitment-only condition were less likely to continue pursuing the job (by participating in the next stage of the selection process) than were applicants who went through a dual purpose interview.

Finally, Stevens (in press) examines interview focus in the context of a campus placement office. Seventy-eight recruiters and 106 applicants responded to surveys about their interviews. In addition, 39 interviews were audiotaped, transcribed, and coded. Stevens found that recruiters whose primary focus was recruitment behaved differently from those who were more selection-oriented: recruitment-oriented recruiters spoke more during the interview, volunteered more information, and asked fewer questions of applicants than other recruiters did. She also found that recruitment-oriented recruiters were less likely than other recruiters to adhere to a strict sequential script. However, Stevens's findings suggest that applicants were not influenced by these variations in behavior: after controlling for pre-interview attraction to the organization, she found no relationship between interview focus and applicant attraction to, or intention to accept a job with, the organization.

Thus findings regarding the impact of interview focus on applicant attraction range from nil, to weak, to counterintuitive. Turban and Dougherty (1992) suggested that the negative relationship between recruitment emphasis and attraction to the job may indicate that applicants were suspicious of jobs that had to be "sold" so extensively. Barber et al. (1994) suggested that applicants who have successfully completed an interview that is at least partially selection-oriented may feel that they have cleared a hurdle, leading to higher expectations of eventually receiving an offer and greater motivation to persist in pursuing the job. Additional research on this topic would have great practical importance, as organizations most likely do not expect recruitment-focused interviews to reduce attraction.

Interview structure. A second aspect of the recruitment interview process that is relevant to applicant attraction is interview structure. Interview structure has a specific meaning in the context of selection. Structured interviews are characterized by systematic construction of interview questions relevant to the job being filled, construction of sample or benchmark responses against which applicants' responses can be compared, and weighting of individual interview questions in terms of their relative importance (Heneman & Heneman, 1994). This preparation, however, is not visible to the applicant who, therefore, cannot determine the degree to which interviews are structured according to selection standards. Instead, applicant assessments of interview structure are likely based on the degree to which the recruiter structures, or controls, the interview. Tullar (1989) defines structuring as "an attempt to restrict the behavioral options of the other person in the conversation while leaving a variety of options open" (p. 971). In this sense, recruiters structure interviews when they dictate (either explicitly or implicitly) the order in which specific issues will be addressed, how much time will be devoted to different segments of the interview, at what point applicants will be allowed to ask questions, and so forth. In practice, the two different forms of structuring may coincide to a great extent: Recruiters who structure interviews in the selection sense of the word probably also structure interviews in the more general sense.

Only two studies have directly assessed relationships between interview structure and applicant reactions. Taylor and Bergmann (1987), in their longitudinal study of recruitment practices of a single company, asked recruiters to assess the degree to which they typically structured their campus interviews. They found that applicants interviewed by recruiters who reported higher levels of interview structure stated higher probabilities of accepting job offers than applicants interviewed by recruiters who were less structured.

Turban and Dougherty (1992), using a placement office sample, also asked recruiters the degree to which they structured interviews. In contrast to Taylor and Bergmann, Turban and Dougherty found no relationship between interview structure and applicant perceptions of organizational attractiveness or probability of receiving a job offer. The different findings may be due to differences in the way structure was measured. Taylor and Bergmann used a single item measure of structure, asking recruiters to indicate the degree to which they structured interviews. It was up to respondents to decide what exactly was meant by interview structure. Turban and Dougherty were more specific, using a scale composed of three items. Recruiters were asked whether they followed a structured format, whether they used a rating scale for candidate responses, and whether they asked the same questions of all candidates. These items focused more clearly on the selection definition of structure and included elements that would not have been apparent to the applicant, which may explain the lack of significant findings.

Interview content. A final aspect of the interview process likely to influence applicant attraction is information content. As noted earlier, applicants generally respond more favorably to recruiters who are perceived as more informative, suggesting that the amount of information provided is important. The question here is whether the type of information provided is also important.

Taylor and Sniezek (1984) provided one of the few studies to address this question directly. They surveyed 148 users of a campus placement office, assessing what was covered during their interviews as well as how they reacted to the interview (specifically, whether they were satisfied that they had had a fair opportunity to present their qualifications, and whether the interview had influenced their evaluation of the organization's attractiveness). Factor analysis of 25 information content items revealed three factors, reflecting general qualifications, specific knowledge (e.g., courses taken), and geographic mobility. Taylor and Sniezek (1984) concluded that applicants reacted positively to interviews that emphasized general qualifications but that they were unaffected by the emphasis placed on specific knowledge or geographic mobility.

A limitation of Taylor and Sniezek's study is that they did not differentiate between information *provided* by the recruiter and information *sought* by the recruiter. Their factor analyses resulted in three dimensions of information that appear to be oriented more toward selection (and the gathering of information) than recruitment (and the dissemination of information). Thus we can say little about what kind of information recruiter should provide. Nonetheless, their results do suggest that topics covered in the interview can influence applicant reactions.

Though Taylor and Sniezek (1984) focused on general content areas and their impact on applicants, an extensive stream of research has examined a different dimension of interview content: its accuracy, or realism. These studies are embedded in the broader literature on realistic job previews, discussed later in this chapter. Therefore they are not reviewed here, but readers with an interest in interview content are strongly encouraged to read the section on realistic previews.

Other factors influencing reactions to the interview. Recently, Stevens (1997) raised an important question regarding reactions to the initial interview. She proposed that applicants' preinterview impressions of a job could influence their reactions to the interview itself through confirmatory information processing. In other words, applicants who hold favorable preinterview impressions might selectively process the information that supports their favorable beliefs, whereas those with negative impressions might focus on less favorable aspects of the recruiter or the interview. If reactions to the interview are strongly influenced by preinterview beliefs, it is unlikely that the initial interview itself can exert much independent influence on applicant reactions. Therefore organizations interested in improving recruitment effectiveness might need to attend to factors that create preinterview impressions rather than focus on the initial interview.

Stevens (1997) provided some evidence in support of this argument. Using both survey data and audiotapes of actual interviews, she demonstrated that preinterview expectancies (beliefs that a job offer would be forthcoming) were positively associated with evaluations of recruiter personableness and informativeness. However, preinterview beliefs about attributes of the job itself were unrelated to evaluations of the recruiter. Further research is needed to corroborate these findings. Such research would be particularly valuable as it would speak to both theoretical and practical issues: it would extend our knowledge of cognitive processing during the interview, while demonstrating clear implications for the effectiveness of different recruitment strategies (e.g., focusing on materials provided prior to the interview rather than on the interview itself.)

Applicant reactions to the interview: Do they really matter? As the above review indicates, there has been a great deal of research on applicant reactions to initial interviews. Evidence generally supports the argument that recruiter traits, such as warmth and informativeness are related to applicant reactions, although these findings are not universal and the effect sizes involved are typically small. The impact of recruiter demographic characteristics on applicant reactions is less well supported. There is some evidence that interview process issues (focus, structure, and content) influence applicant reactions, but this conclusion is based on relatively few findings and additional research into these issues is warranted. Furthermore, at least one study concluded that the impact of recruiter characteristics on applicant reactions deteriorates over time, having stronger impact immediately after the interview than later during the recruitment process (Taylor & Bergmann, 1987).

Given small effect sizes and the possible transitory impact of initial interviews on applicant reactions, it is reasonable to ask whether these findings—indeed, this area of research—are particularly important. In answering this question, one must be careful about what is expected. Although the effects of any single aspect of the interview (e.g., a particular recruiter trait, a specific process issue) are likely to be small, the cumulative effects of multiple aspects of the interview may be substantial. For example, Turban and Dougherty (1992) included a fairly comprehensive set of interview factors in their study, and found that as a set they accounted for 26% of the variance in hire expectancies and 32% of the variance in overall attraction. Effects such as these may well have substantial practical importance, particularly in competitive labor markets. In addition, we should be reluctant to dismiss these effects as unimportant because they might be transitory in nature. If immediate reactions to the interview cause applicants to withdraw from the recruitment process, then those immediate reactions are not transitory but final; applicants are not likely to re-enter the process at a later date. For applicants who have withdrawn, later decisions are moot, as they have in effect already rejected any potential job offer.

Context Issues: When does the interview matter? Of course, it is also possible that the importance of initial interview effects on applicant attraction varies across situations. Three potential moderators of the interview—attraction relationship have been proposed and examined (Rynes, et al., 1980; Taylor & Bergmann, 1987):

1. It has been suggested that offer comparability moderates the impact of initial interviews on applicant attraction. When applicants must choose from a set of offers that are comparable with respect to objective or subjective characteristics, initial recruiting experiences may become important as a "tie-breaker." Decisions may be based on recruiters and interview processes when other information fails to differentiate offers (Behling, et al., 1968).

2. Work experience may moderate the impact of recruitment. More experienced employees would be more aware of the importance of job and organizational attributes, relative to the recruitment process, in determining their ultimate satisfaction with a job. Therefore, they would be more likely to attend to job characteristics, and less likely to attend to recruitment, in evaluating a job opportunity (Rynes, et al., 1980).

3. Labor market opportunities might moderate the relationship between initial interview experiences and applicant attraction. Applicants who have a greater number of job opportunities are less constrained in their choice than those with fewer options. Therefore, they may be more able to use initial interview experiences as a distinguishing factor (Taylor & Bergmann, 1987).

Empirical research provides little support for these context effects. Taylor and Bergmann, as well as Harris and Fink, examined whether the comparability (or relative attractiveness) of job offers moderated the recruitment- attraction relationship. Neither study found evidence to support this effect.

Rynes et al. (1991) reported exploratory evidence suggesting that applicants with less full-time work experience were more susceptible to recruiter influence. Taylor and Bergmann, as well as Harris and Fink, explicitly tested this hypothesis, however, and found no evidence of moderation. Harris and Fink, as well as Turban & Dougherty, tested for the experience effect using a slightly different operationalization of experience: job search experience rather than work experience per se. Again, however, no evidence of moderation was found.

The effect of alternative job opportunities was studied directly by Liden and Parsons (1986), Harris and Fink, as well as Taylor and Bergmann. Of these, only Liden and Parsons found significant effects. In their study, the relationship between general reactions to the interview and job acceptance intentions was moderated by the perception of alternative opportunities. Although they did not explicitly interpret this interaction in their paper, one might presume that it was consistent with their hypothesis: Those with more perceived alternatives were more influenced by general reactions to the interview. In addition, Maurer et al. (1992) found that the relationship between reactions to the interview process and likelihood of offer acceptance was stronger among engineering graduates in the top quartile of their cohort with respect to grade point average than among students in the bottom quartile. To the extent that students with higher grades receive more offers (or expect to receive more offers), this finding provides indirect support for the anticipated moderation.

Similarly, Stevens (1997) found that applicants who expected to receive many job offers were more likely to be influenced by initial interviews than applicants who expected to receive fewer total offers. Thus, what little evidence of moderation exists suggests that the effects of initial recruitment may be strongest among the most sought-after applicants, a finding that increases the practical importance of initial recruitment activities.

Recruiter-Centered Research

The literature reviewed above regarding applicant reactions to initial interviews is relatively rich. The question has been addressed using a variety of methods, a number of contextual factors have been considered, and underlying processes have been assessed (though to a limited degree). The net result of this research is to suggest that the way the recruiter conducts him- or herself during initial recruitment contacts can influence applicant attraction.

In contrast, there is almost no literature, conceptual or empirical, that examines recruiter perspectives on the initial interview. Rather, recruiter behaviors are taken as given, and recruiters themselves are treated as passive actors. Almost no attention is paid to recruiter goals, motivation, training, or any other factor that might determine how recruiters conduct themselves during this initial recruitment contact. This is particularly unfortunate given that recruiters have a great deal of discretion with respect to their behaviors. Indeed, anecdotes detailing offensive and inappropriate recruiter behavior, such as those reported in Rynes et al. (1991), suggest that there is substantial room for improvement in recruiter performance.

Recruiter motivation: The goals of initial recruitment. Human behavior is generally goal-oriented. Therefore one factor that might have significant impact on recruiters' behavior is how they identify or construe the goals of the recruitment interview.

In many cases, the organization represented by the recruiter will have multiple goals for the initial interview. As noted earlier, these interviews typically serve at least two purposes, selection and recruitment. In addition, there may be "public relations" goals that are unrelated to recruitment or selection of specific candidates. For example, it is not unheard of for organizations to conduct initial interviews even when they have no openings, in order to maintain visibility within a particular applicant population. Possible spillover effects that might result when applicants report their interview experiences to potential customers, investors, or future applicants add to the public relations dimension of initial recruitment contacts.

A reasonable starting point in assessing recruiter goals is to consider the organization's goals, with the presumption that the recruiter will carry out the goals of his or her employer. Unfortunately, we know essentially nothing about how organizations set goals for recruitment interviews. As suggested earlier, it seems likely that organizations will emphasize recruitment over selection when hiring needs are great and candidates scarce, and will emphasize selection over recruitment when there are many applicants for few jobs. Furthermore, it seems probable that organizations with strong and positive images will be less concerned about public relations issues than organizations that are either less well known or less attractive. However, these are mere speculations that await empirical confirmation.

It is also unclear how effectively organizational goals are transmitted to the recruiters themselves. First, evidence obtained from some of the U.S.'s largest corporations suggests that minimal training is provided to recruiters (Rynes & Boudreau, 1986). They simply may not know what the organization's goals are. Second, we cannot assume that recruiters share their organization's goals. This issue can perhaps best be understood by reference to agency theory (e.g., Eisenhart, 1989). Recruiters are agents hired to carry out the organization's agenda (be it recruitment, selection, public relations, or some combination of the three). However, they likely have their own goals and objectives that may or may not coincide with those of the organization. For example, they might misunderstand or disagree with the organization's desired emphasis on selection, recruitment, or public relations. Alternatively, they might be motivated to hire people from their alma mater, either to be a loyal supporter of the school or to build a political power base within the organization. Or, they could be motivated to wield power over applicants, or to be popular with applicants, or to have an enjoyable break in their regular work routine. Because it is very difficult for the organization to monitor the behaviors of recruiters (particularly those who conduct initial interviews away from the organization's premises), there is substantial risk that recruiters will attempt to fulfill their own goals rather than those of the organization.

Understanding recruiters' goals is important because it may shed substantial light on recruiter behaviors. In addition, if organizational and recruiter goals are found to diverge, methods for realigning those goals and ensuring recruiter behavior consistent with organizational goals can be examined. For instance, if recruiters simply are unaware of organizational goals, additional training is an appropriate remedy. Alternatively, if recruiters as agents find it more beneficial to pursue their own goals than those of the organization, incentive systems that align recruiter and organization goals (Asch, 1990) might be effective.

Recruiter skills: Can training make recruiters more effective? As discussed above, recruiter motivation likely has a substantial impact on how recruiters conduct initial interviews. The ability of recruiters to tailor their behavior to meet either their own or organizational goals, however, depends on their knowledge of, and ability to carry out, behaviors that will help them achieve those goals. Rynes and Boudreau (1986) found that many Fortune 500 firms provided no training for recruiters, and that those that did offer training provided on average only 13 hours. There have been numerous calls for research examining the benefits of recruiter training, and specific proposals regarding the appropriate form such training should take have been offered (e.g., Maurer, et al., 1992; Rynes & Barber, 1990; Stevens, et al., 1990). Certainly, the practical value of the research reviewed above would be enhanced if we could demonstrate that training programs designed on the basis of that research led to enhanced recruitment effectiveness.

Two studies provide evidence on the influence of recruiter training. Taylor and Bergmann (1987), in a field study of the recruitment practices of a single organization, found no association between recruiters' reports of whether they had received interview training and applicants' post-interview attraction to the organization. Stevens (in press), in a cross-organizational study conducted in a campus placement setting, found that recruiters who had been trained behaved differently from untrained recruiters: they asked more open-ended questions, more follow-up questions, and more performance- differentiating questions (i.e., questions to which the "correct" answer is not obvious) than untrained recruiters. Trained recruiters were also less likely to discuss non-job-related issues than untrained recruiters. Stevens, however, did not find any evidence that these different behaviors influenced applicant attraction to the organization or intentions to accept a job with the organization.

Unfortunately, neither of these studies provides information about the nature of the training provided to those who were trained. It is quite possible (and indeed, seems probable, on the basis of Stevens's results) that the training provided focused on selection aspects of the interview rather than recruitment aspects. If this is the case, the lack of recruitment effects is not terribly surprising. Future research on this topic should clearly identify the content of the training received.

Of course, formal training is not the only approach to improving recruiter skills. Performance management systems that provide recruiters with feedback regarding the effectiveness of their efforts present an alternative to formal training. Rynes and Boudreau's (1986) findings, however, do not suggest that developmental performance appraisals are used in lieu of training to improve recruiter skills. They found that few companies tracked recruitment results, either overall or for specific recruiters, and that individual performance rewards were not strongly tied to recruitment performance. Indeed, taken as a whole, the results reported by Rynes and Boudreau indicate that recruiters are not effectively managed at all. Whether these same results would be obtained in other samples (i.e., the service sector, smaller firms) or if more current data were collected is unknown, and replication of their findings is needed. Assuming their findings can be replicated at least to a degree, however, future research might then focus on ascertaining why so little attention is paid to recruiter management, and on designing and testing programs for improving recruiter performance.

Interactive Models of the Recruitment Interview

One characteristic of this second phase of recruitment that distinguishes it from the phase reviewed in the previous chapter is that recruitment activities during this phase typically involve face-to-face interaction. This creates a dynamic environment in which each party has the opportunity to influence the other. Such dynamism is certainly characteristic of the employment interview. As a result, many have called for research on the interview to take an interactionist perspective (Herriot, 1993; Taylor & Giannantonio, 1993), simultaneously considering both applicant and recruiter. As expressed by Herriot (1993):

> Clearly, information is being processed by both parties, and how each processes the information provided by the other's behavior affects how each behaves and consequently is perceived. (p. 372)

At least two patterns of effects can be studied from the interactionist perspective. First, one could assess whether applicant characteristics and behavior influence recruiter behavior, and whether recruiter behavior then in turn influences applicant attraction to the organization. Second, one could study whether recruiter characteristics and behavior influence applicant behavior, and whether in turn applicant behavior influences selection decisions. As the second question is more relevant to selection than to recruitment, however, I focus on the first.

To date, relatively few studies have examined recruitment issues from the perspective of both applicants and recruiters. Macan and Dipboye (1990), in a field study conducted in a campus placement office, examined (1) how recruiters' pre-interview assessments of applicant qualifications affected their conduct of the interview, and (2) whether applicant perceptions that they were favorably evaluated by the recruiter were related to attraction to the organization. They found that applicants who believed they had been favorably evaluated were more likely to hold positive impressions of the interviewer, the job, and the organization. These applicants, however, were not more likely to state that they intended to accept an offer if they received one.

Macan and Dipboye also found that recruiters did not alter their conduct of the interview in response to applicant qualifications. They did not spend more time with highly qualified candidates nor did they change interview focus. These results are consistent with the findings of Tullar (1989). Tullar analyzed videotapes of actual recruitment interviews of successful and unsuccessful job candidates. He found that successful applicants and unsuccessful applicants behaved differently during the interview but that recruiter behavior did not change as a function of the applicant.

In another interactive study, Powell and Goulet (1996) provided evidence that is at least suggestive of applicant impact on recruiter behavior. They found that applicants were able to predict recruiters' intentions regarding whether to extend invitations for second interviews and job offers, which may be evidence that recruiters do behave differently when they evaluate an applicant favorably. But these findings do not provide unambiguous support for interactive effects, as it is unclear to what extent these predictions were based primarily on recruiter behavior during the interview and to what extent they were due to applicants' assessments of their own objective qualifications.

Stevens (1997), in a study of campus placement interviews, found that applicants' pre-interview expectancies (i.e., beliefs about the probability that they would be offered a job by this organization) were associated with applicants' behavior. An analysis combining self-report survey data with transcribed audiotapes of actual interviews suggested that applicants who expected to receive an offer engaged in more impression management behaviors than applicants who were more pessimistic about their chances. This pattern introduces the possibility of self-fulfilling prophecies in the interview: the behavior of more confident applicants might elicit favorable or supportive behaviors from the recruiter. Stevens, however, found no evidence of this pattern and, for that matter, little evidence that applicant behaviors influenced recruiter behaviors at all.

In short, these few investigations of interaction during the interview do not provide strong support for reciprocal influences. As Macan and Dipboye (1990) noted, the ritualistic context of college placement interviews (in which the above research was conducted) may reduce the likelihood that interactive effects will emerge. Situational constraints may cause recruiters to avoid varying their behavior in response to applicant characteristics or behaviors. For example, recruiters may be attempting to follow predetermined interview structures or, for that matter, to adhere to inflexible interview schedules. Alternatively, they may be concerned about negative public relations consequences associated with summarily dismissing less qualified applicants. Additional research into recruiter perspectives on the interview, as recommended above, could prove useful in determining why recruiter behavior does not appear to vary in response to applicant characteristics and behavior in campus recruitment settings, and might also shed light on whether such effects would emerge in other contexts.

Recruitment and Attraction
After the Initial Interview

As mentioned earlier in this chapter, the second stage of recruitment is quite broad and encompasses a number of decisions on the applicant's part. The bulk of the existing research deals with the initial screening interview, associating this rather early interaction either with nonbehavioral outcomes (e.g., attraction to the organization) or with relatively distal behavioral outcomes (e.g., the decision to accept a job offer if one is made). In reality, though, for most applicants (including college graduates, the focus of much of the recruitment interview research), the behavioral outcome that immediately follows the initial interview is a decision about whether to continue to pursue the job. A decision to pursue means that the applicant will become involved in later recruitment and selection events, which I define as any applicant-organization interaction that follows the initial screening interview but precedes extension of a job offer. Later events include site visits (i.e., extended interviews conducted at the employer's site), selection procedures (e.g., physical or psychological tests, drug testing, reference checks), and administrative procedures (e.g., coordinating site visits and selection procedures, providing the applicant with information about his or her status as a candidate).

These later activities generally require a significant commitment of time and energy on the part of the applicant, both because they are inherently more time consuming than initial interviews and because they may require the applicant to travel to the new work site or to other company offices. Because the cost of pursuing employment past the initial interview can be significant, applicants have an incentive to screen carefully before committing themselves to continued pursuit. Once they have made the decision to pursue, however, applicants are quite likely to be influenced by later recruitment experiences. These events might be expected to influence applicant attraction to the organization for the same reasons initial interviews might have an effect. First, applicants may consider their experiences during these events as indicators of how the organization likely would treat them later, or may view the people with whom they interact during these events as representative of future coworkers. In other words, these later recruitment experiences may serve as signals (Spence, 1973, 1974) of what the organization is really like. Second, applicants may make inferences about their probability of receiving a job offer on the basis of these experiences. And third, applicants may respond to the demographic makeup of individuals they meet during these later contacts, either because of personal biases regarding the kind of individuals they prefer to work with (Rynes, 1991) or because they are more easily influenced by others similar to themselves (Maurer, et al., 1992).

In this section, I review two issues relevant to later recruitment events: how applicants decide whether to participate in those events, and how specific aspects of later recruitment (specifically, site visits, administrative procedures, and selection techniques) influence applicant decisions.

The Decision to Pursue Jobs
Past the Initial Interview

Despite the voluminous literature on reactions to initial screening interviews, few studies have dealt explicitly with the decision to continue to pursue employment by engaging in later recruitment activities. Therefore we know little about how these decisions are made. Two studies addressed this issue. Rynes et al. (1991) examined decisions to accept or reject site visit invitations. They found that 28 of 41 subjects in a longitudinal interview study had rejected site visit invitations, most commonly because the invitation had come too late or because the job opportunity was not sufficiently attractive. In addition, three applicants rejected site visits because of experiences with recruiters during the initial interview stage. Barber et al. (1994), in a field experiment, found that one third of the initial applicants withdrew from the selection process following initial interviews, and that withdrawal rates were higher among applicants who had been exposed to an interview focused exclusively on recruitment (rather than selection). They were, however, able to explain only a small percentage of the variance in withdrawal.

What these studies suggest is that applicants frequently do withdraw from hiring processes following initial interviews. As a result, they suggest that examination of exactly who withdraws, and under what circumstances, warrants further consideration. At least two possible reasons for applicant withdrawal should be considered. First, applicants may withdraw because the job opportunity has become less attractive to them relative to their other options. This perspective is central to recruitment and underlies much of the research discussed in this book. Organizations are likely to respond to this type of withdrawal by attempting to make their positions more attractive. An alternative view, one more common in the job search literature, is that applicant withdrawal is driven by applicants' mental states. Continued pursuit of employment requires persistence, and persistence can vary as a function of many factors, including self-esteem (Ellis & Taylor, 1983) and self-efficacy (Eden & Aviram, 1993). In particular, applicants who believe they are unlikely to receive a job offer may withdraw in order to avoid anticipated rejection. Though it is unclear whether organizations would want to eliminate this sort of withdrawal, a number of studies have demonstrated that it can be avoided through interventions aimed at providing social and emotional support to job seekers (e.g., Eden & Aviram, 1993; Vinokur, van Ryn, Gramlich, & Price, 1991). In any event, a complete understanding of applicant withdrawal during this phase of recruitment requires consideration of both perspectives.

Applicant Reactions to Later Recruitment Events

Applicants' experiences during later aspects of the recruitment process are likely to be particularly salient for at least three reasons. First, they occur closer in time to the job choice decision; second, they involve a greater variety of organizational actors and therefore may be seen as more representative of the organization as a whole than an interview with a single individual might be; and third, these interactions are longer and more intense than are earlier recruitment interactions (Taylor & Bergmann, 1987). Despite the probable significance of these events, however, they have been the focus of little research. A few studies investigating the impact of site visits and administrative procedures (specifically, time lags and delays) are reviewed below.

Applicant Reactions to Site Visits

Three studies have investigated applicant reactions to site visits: two field studies conducted within a single organization, and one interview study cutting across organizations. In the former category, Taylor & Bergmann (1987) examined applicant perceptions of how well they were treated by their host, whether they had sufficient opportunities to interact with others during the site visit, and what sort of evaluation procedures they went through during their site visit. They found no evidence that these factors influenced general attraction to the organization or applicants' probability of accepting a job if offered one. They also failed to find any evidence that the amount of information provided about site visit logistics (e.g., schedule, transportation) influenced applicant reactions.

Turban, Campion, and Eyring (1995) also examined applicant reactions to their site visits in the context of a single company. Specifically, they investigated whether previsit information regarding logistics of the trip itself, the amount of information provided during site visit, overall evaluations of the visit, or perceptions of host characteristics (e.g., helpfulness, likeableness) influenced job acceptance intentions or job acceptance decisions. They found that overall evaluations of the site visit had small effect on job acceptance intentions, and a somewhat stronger effect on actual decisions. In addition, host likeableness was positively associated with acceptance intentions and decisions but host helpfulness was negatively related to acceptance intentions.

The two studies described above each dealt with applicant reactions to the later recruitment practices of a single company. One potential limitation of this within-firm approach is that there may have been significant restriction of range in the site visit process variables. If site visit arrangements and assessment procedures are centrally managed, there may be little variation in these factors, reducing their observed impact on dependent variables. Turban et al. addressed this issue, pointing out that recruitment practices within the organization they studied were in fact quite decentralized. Even so, it is likely that variation in recruitment practices within a company is constrained relative to the variation that might be found across companies, and therefore the null findings of the studies described above should be interpreted with some caution.

A third study, Rynes et al. (1991), assessed applicant reactions to the recruitment practices of a variety of companies. Collecting data via in-depth interviews, they found that almost one third of their subjects rejected offers from companies they had initially favored due at least in part to site visit experiences. Critical factors in applicants' evaluation of the site visit included the status of people met during the visit, whether applicants felt "specially treated," whether the company had been flexible in scheduling the visit, and whether the visit had been conducted in a professional manner.

One aspect of the site visit that has surprisingly not been explored is the impact of the demographic composition of organizational members met during the visit on applicant reactions. This omission is surprising given the amount of attention paid to the demographic characteristics of campus recruiters. If the campus recruiter is expected to serve as a signal of organizational diversity and/or the role of minority individuals in the organization, one would also expect the degree of diversity actually observed at the organization to send such signals. Despite growing interest in organizational demography, to my knowledge only one study has examined its relationship to recruitment, and that study (Jackson, Brett, Sessa, Cooper, Julin, & Peyronnin, 1991) focused on whether recruitment practices (specifically, internal recruitment) caused demographic homogeneity. Certainly, this issue merits investigation from an applicant attraction standpoint.

Applicant Reactions to Time Lags and Delays

Studies examining reactions to site visits have included some elements of administrative procedures, such as travel arrangements. Another recruitment administration issue that has received research attention is the effect of time lags or communication delays on applicant attraction. Arvey, Gordon, Massengill and Mussio (1975) studied the impact of delays between initial application and subsequent screening on both majority and minority applicants. Time lags were expected to be associated with applicant dropouts for two reasons. First, as more time passed between initial application and subsequent testing, the likelihood that an alternative job would be accepted would increase. Second, as time passed, applicant expectations of receiving an offer would decline. Arvey et al. found that time lags were associated with higher drop out rates. They also found this effect to be stronger among minority applicants than among majority applicants. More recently, however, Taylor and Bergmann (1987) found no evidence of association between delays and applicant reactions.

Rynes et al. (1991) found that many applicants (39 of their 41 subjects) experienced lengthy delays during the recruitment process. Further, of those 39 who felt they had experienced substantial delays, 20 stated that the delay had "definitely" influenced their willingness to accept a position with the company and an additional 11 said it had "somewhat" influenced their willingness to accept. Rynes et al. (1991) further suggested that these numbers may underestimate the actual impact of delays, as delays might have an indirect effect by giving time, for example, for other (potentially more attractive) offers to be received. These authors also examined the mechanisms by which delays influenced application reactions. They found that applicants tended to attribute delays to their own undesirability as candidates (28/39) or to organizational incompetence (20/39). Those making internal attributions tended to be somewhat less qualified than those making organizational attributions.

Applicant Reactions to Selection Procedures

To a great extent, recruitment and selection occur simultaneously, and it is extremely difficult to disentangle their effects. Selection system utility depends on the quality of candidates in the applicant pool (Boudreau & Rynes, 1985) and therefore depends on effective recruitment. Furthermore, as a growing body of research has demonstrated, selection procedures can influence applicant attitudes in ways that have implications for both selection and recruitment. Smither, Reilly, Millsap, Pearlman, & Stoffey (1993) identified a number of possible consequences of applicant reactions to selection procedures. First, they suggested that selection procedures that are considered offensive or inappropriate may lead to discrimination complaints and court challenges. Second, they argued that applicant reactions can influence the validity of selection devices, in that low motivation to perform on a test that is perceived to be unfair could result in biased or inaccurate scores. Finally, and most germane to recruitment, applicant reactions to selection procedures may influence whether applicants pursue or accept job offers, and may also have spillover effects on other applicants.

The notion that selection processes can influence job applicants is not new. For example, research into applicant reactions to interviews (which are typically selection procedures as well as recruitment devices) has a long history, as reviewed in detail above. And Schmidt, Greenthal, Hunter, Berner and Seaton (1977) cited studies of applicant reactions to selection procedures dating as far back as 1945. Early evidence of applicant reactions to selection procedures appeared in studies intended to address other issues. For example, Schmidt et al. (1977) focused primarily on the amount of adverse impact associated with two forms of tests: job sample (performance) tests and written tests. In a sample of 87 metal trades apprentices, they found that content-valid job sample tests had less adverse impact than paper-and-pencil tests. They also found that both minority and majority test-takers considered the job sample tests to be more fair, more clear, and more appropriate in terms of difficulty than written tests. The study did not address whether these different reactions were associated with different levels of attraction to the organization (nor would it have made sense to do so, as the apprentices were already employed).

Cascio and Phillips (1979) focused on a variety of performance tests (defined as tests involving demonstrations of behaviors). A total of 21 tests, including both motor and verbal tests, were examined. Here, the focus was on the usefulness of the performance tests in selecting city government employees. Their reliability, adverse impact, and cost effectiveness were assessed. Cascio and Phillips also provided indirect evidence of employee reactions to the performance tests. Complaints filed about testing procedures dropped to zero when the previously used written tests were replaced with performance tests. Again, however, no direct assessment of the impact of testing procedures on applicant attraction was made.

More recently, a number of studies have focused directly on reactions to selection procedures, examining which procedures are viewed most favorably (e.g., Rosse, Miller & Stecher, 1994; Rynes & Connerly, 1993; Smither, et al., 1993; Steiner & Gilliland, 1996). Rynes and Connerly (1993) asked a sample of 390 university students (from one midwestern and one northeastern university) to indicate how 13 selection procedures would influence their attraction to an organization. They found that simulation-based interviews, reference tests, and business-related tests were more likely to result in attraction, while psychological tests, "generic" (unstructured) interviews, and handwriting analyses generated the least favorable reactions. Similarly, Steiner and Gilliland (1996) asked French and U.S. college students to assess the favorability of 10 selection procedures. Both groups rated interviews, resumes, and work-sample tests quite highly, whereas honesty tests, personal contacts, and handwriting analyses were viewed with disfavor.

Do Selection Procedures
Influence Recruitment Outcomes?

The studies described above suggest that applicants do react to selection procedures, in the general sense that some procedures are viewed more favorably than others. Whether these affective reactions translate into behaviors relevant to recruitment, such as dropping out of the applicant pool or rejecting a job if one is offered, is a separate issue. There are, however, both conceptual and empirical reasons to believe that such effects may occur.

On a conceptual level, two frameworks for explaining applicant reactions to selection procedures have emerged. The first is based on privacy concerns and suggests that applicants will resist procedures that do not allow them to control sensitive personal information about themselves (Stone & Stone, 1990). The second is based on justice concerns, and argues that selection procedures will be viewed more favorably to the extent that they are viewed as just in terms of both process and outcome (Gilliland, 1993). An inductive study of applicant reactions to selection procedures conducted by Rynes and Connerly (1993) provided indirect support for both of these frameworks. Rynes and Connerly (1993) identified three major considerations driving applicant reactions: perceived likelihood that procedures are accurate (reflecting a concern for procedural justice), whether the employer was thought to need the information acquired (a possible reflection of privacy concerns) and how well the applicant thought he or she would do on the test (a distributive justice concern).

Identification of the factors underlying reactions to selection procedures helps clarify their likely impact on recruitment outcomes. Privacy and justice are important employment issues, and their relevance extends well beyond recruitment and selection. Applicants therefore might interpret the degree to which selection techniques are fair and protect (or invade) their privacy as indicators of how organizations will treat them as employees; in other words, a signaling effect (Spence, 1973, 1974) may exist.

On the empirical level, several studies have assessed whether applicant reactions to selection procedures are related to recruitment outcomes. Both direct outcomes (i.e, the applicant's own attraction to the organization) and indirect, or spillover, outcomes (including the applicant's willingness to recommend the organization as an employer and willingness to purchase the organization's product) have been considered.

Crant and Bateman (1990) conducted a study of reactions to drug testing that explicitly considered recruitment and attraction outcomes. In their study, 163 undergraduate students read descriptions of a potential employer that were experimentally varied in terms of (a) whether or not a drug-testing program was in place and (b) whether organizational data (e.g., absenteeism, accident rates) suggested that a drug testing program might be needed. After reviewing the descriptions, students were asked to indicate their overall evaluation of the company and the likelihood that they would apply for a job with the company. Crant and Bateman found that the students had more favorable attitudes toward companies that did not test for drug use, and also were more inclined to apply for jobs with such companies.

Smither et al. (1993) assessed the reactions of 460 civil service job applicants to actual screening procedures. The procedures used consisted of different exams for different jobs, but all consisted of multiple choice knowledge or ability tests. Immediately after taking the test, applicants completed an instrument measuring their attraction to the organization. Three months later, applicants responded to questions about the likelihood that they would recommend this employer to other job seekers. This study indicated that attraction to the organization was positively related to reactions to the tests, as was willingness to recommend the employer to others.

Macan, Avedon, Paese, & Smith (1994) assessed applicant reactions to cognitive tests and to assessment centers. Their sample consisted of

3984 manufacturing employees who took cognitive tests and 194 (a subset of the original sample) who also participated in an assessment center. Reactions to the cognitive tests were positively associated with organizational attractiveness and with intentions to accept the job. Reactions to the tests were only weakly related to intentions to purchase the company's products (an assessment of spillover). Data from the subsample that also participated in the assessment center indicated that perceptions of the assessment center were positively related to organizational attractiveness and intentions to accept the offer, but again only weakly related to intentions to purchase the company's product.

In summary, employee reactions to selection procedures is a growing and promising area of research, with implications for both recruitment and selection. At this point, several lines of research seem most promising for those whose primary interest is recruitment. First, conceptual arguments about the importance of privacy and justice as determinants of reactions should be used to predict employee reactions to specific types of selection devices. To date, most research on this topic has explored individual differences in reactions to selection procedures (e.g., Smither, et al., 1993) or has examined reactions to different modes of using a single procedure (e.g., Gilliland, 1994). From an organizational recruitment standpoint, however, it might be most useful to know whether selection procedures can be categorized according to their perceived justice or invasiveness. A natural extension of such research would be to examine whether these categorizations could be used to select procedures that are likely to yield better recruitment outcomes. An important caveat is provided by the findings of Chan and his colleagues, however, whose work (e.g., Chan, 1997; Chan, et al., 1997) suggests that there may be significant racial differences in test reactions. Because fair employment and workforce diversity remain important aspects of organizational recruitment, recruitment researchers need to remain sensitive to the possibility that evaluations of selection procedures may vary across groups.

Communication Realism During Recruitment

One of the more critical decisions that organizations must make about their recruitment practices involves the accuracy, or realism, of the information they provide. One approach is to "sell" the job and the organization, by portraying them in the most favorable light; in other words, by emphasizing positive features and disregarding negative features. A second approach is to provide complete and balanced information about the job, revealing both positive and negative features. Programs intended to deliver such balanced information are known as "realistic job previews" or RJPs. An extensive stream of recruitment research has focused on the relative merits of RJPs versus traditional "selling" approaches. This material is reviewed below.

RJP Effects

The use of RJPs has been recommended because they are expected to lead to a variety of positive outcomes for the organization, including higher job satisfaction, commitment, and performance, as well as lower turnover. RJPs may also have immediate effects on recruitment outcomes in that the provision of negative information may reduce applicants' willingness to accept the job. Wanous (1992) argued that the primary objective of RJPs is to reduce turnover, and most RJP research reflects this priority.

Breaugh (1983) summarized the four mechanisms by which RJPs are expected to influence turnover: met expectations, ability to cope, air of honesty/commitment, and self-selection. First, RJPs are supposed to reduce turnover by lowering initial job expectations to a level consistent with actual job experience. Employees whose pre-hire expectations are met are more likely to remain on the job; employees whose pre-hire expectations are not met are likely to be dissatisfied with the job and ultimately to leave it. Second, employees who know what challenges to expect from a job may develop coping skills that help them meet those challenges, perhaps by planning in advance how they will respond. Third, recipients of realistic previews may feel more committed to employers who provide them with realistic information because they appreciate the employers' honesty and because their decision to accept the job was based on complete information. Finally, RJPs may lead to applicant self-selection: Applicants who are not likely to be satisfied with the job will not accept job offers, and those who do accept will therefore be more likely to remain.

Research addressing whether RJPs reduce turnover has been reviewed in detail elsewhere, in both narrative and quantitative form (e.g., McEvoy & Cascio, 1985; Premack & Wanous, 1985; Reilly, Brown, Blood, & Malatesta, 1981; Rynes, 1991; Wanous & Collela, 1989; Wanous, 1992). In general, these reviews suggest that RJPs influence turnover but that the effect is modest. For example, a meta-analysis of 21 studies conducted by Premack and Wanous (1985) found that the corrected mean correlation between information realism and turn-over was 0.12, and McEvoy and Cascio's (1985) meta-analysis of 15 studies concluded that the corrected mean correlation was 0.18.

Whether this effect is practically important is largely a matter of perspective. For instance, Rynes (1991) argued that the effect is mod-est, and that it is probably overwhelmed by actual on-the-job experi-ences. Irving and Meyer (1994) drew similar conclusions, suggesting that organizations "should focus on providing new recruits with positive work experiences rather than on confirming their preentry expectations" (p. 948). And McEvoy and Cascio (1985) pointed out that job enrichment interventions were about twice as effective as RJPs in reducing turnover. Certainly, there are many factors that influence turnover, and therefore it would not be reasonable to expect the magnitude of RJP effects to be extremely large. An evaluation of the usefulness of RJPs, however, should consider not just their effect on turnover but also their cost effectiveness. RJPs can be an inexpensive means to achieve some reduction in turnover, in most cases requiring far fewer resources than would be needed to alter new hires' experience of work. If the returns associated with the use of RJPs exceed their costs (see Premack & Wanous, 1985, for examples of these calcula-tions), then they may be deemed successful, even if their effects on turnover are not large.

These reviews also addressed whether RJP effects are consistent across situations. Breaugh (1983) argued that RJPs are likely to be effective in reducing turnover only under certain conditions: For example, when applicants can choose from among multiple job offers, when applicants have unrealistic expectations, or when applicants would have difficulty coping with job demands in the absence of a realistic preview. The two meta-analyses published in 1985 reached different conclusions as to whether such contingencies are likely to be important. McEvoy and Cascio (1985) concluded that there was suf-ficient residual variance across studies to warrant examination of possible contingency factors; Premack and Wanous concluded that there was not. More recently, however, Wanous (1992) proposed a number of conditions under which realistic previews are more likely to be effective (e.g., when job opportunities are plentiful, when accu-rate information about the job is difficult to obtain, or both). This suggests a general consensus that RJP effects do vary across situations.

Since 1985, several new studies have added to our understanding of the effects of RJPs on turnover. Suszko and Breaugh (1986) studied the effect of a combination of written and oral RJPs on a sample of 28 individuals applying for the position of inventory taker. Half received realistic information and half did not. As expected, Suszko and Breaugh (1986) found less voluntary turnover among RJP subjects than among control group subjects.

Meglino, DeNisi, Youngblood, & Williams (1988), in a longitudinal experiment involving 533 U.S. Army trainees, examined the effects of two different types of previews: one designed to reduce overly optimistic expectations (traditional RJP, called by the authors a reduction preview), and one designed to raise overly pessimistic expectations (called an enhancement preview). They found that subjects exposed to a combination of reduction and enhancement previews, and subjects exposed to an enhancement preview only, had lower turnover than subjects in a control group, but that exposure to the reduction preview alone actually was associated with higher turnover. They also found that RJPs were more effective in reducing turnover among more intelligent and more committed applicants.

Meglino, DeNisi & Ravlin (1993) studied the impact of RJPs on 1117 corrections officer applicants. An experimental group saw a videotaped RJP; a control group did not. Meglino et al. (1993) found no overall retention effects. Among those with previous exposure to the job, however, the RJP was associated with lower turnover during a probationary period but with higher turnover thereafter.

In summary, these three newer studies provide additional support for the effect of RJPs on turnover. The latter two studies also suggest that the effect is not consistent across individuals: effects appear to be stronger among more intelligent, more committed, and (in the short term) more experienced applicants.

It is interesting to note that while these studies examined how *individual*-characteristics moderate RJP effectiveness, very few studies have addressed how *RJP*-characteristics moderate RJP effectiveness, particularly with respect to turnover. One study that did address this topic is Colarelli's (1984) study of turnover among bank tellers. Colarelli systematically altered whether applicants received realistic job information from a brochure or from an incumbent teller. (A control group received no RJP.) He found that turnover was lower for individuals who received RJP information from job incumbents than for either individuals who received the same information via a brochure or individuals who received no RJP at all.

Since then, research into the consequences of variations in RJP format and design has all but ceased. In part, this may be the result of Premack and Wanous's (1985) conclusion that there was not enough residual variance in turnover across RJP studies to warrant a search for moderators. But as Rynes (1991) noted, Premack and Wanous's results were based on a fairly small number of studies and may not have had sufficient power to detect significant moderator effects. Furthermore, evidence that individual characteristics moderate RJP effectiveness (described above) suggests that other forms of moderation might also be possible. Therefore, research into the consequences of RJP design choices such as presentation format, timing of the RJP (i.e., whether the realistic information is provided early or late in the recruitment cycle), specific topics addressed, and information sources used (e.g., job incumbent versus human resource staff person) might help identify RJP "best practices," that is, ways to administer RJPs that maximize their effects on turnover. Such questions could be addressed by means of individual studies in which RJP characteristics are systematically varied (similar to Colarelli, 1984). Alternatively, existing research could be meta-analyzed to see whether RJP design factors account for significant variance across studies.

Theoretical Rationale for RJP Effects

Rynes (1991) and Wanous (1992) called for more attention to the processes underlying RJP effects on turnover. In this section, research pertaining to three of the four mechanisms (met expectations, commitment, and air of honesty) is reviewed. Discussion of self-selection effects is deferred to the following section because of its unique implications for applicant attraction.

In their 1985 meta-analysis, Premack and Wanous (1985) summarized existing research on the met expectations hypothesis, and concluded that the corrected mean correlation between realism of preview and level of expectations was -0.17. This finding supports the notion that RJPs reduce inflated expectations. They also found a positive relationship between preview realism and post-hire job satisfaction, providing further support for this hypothesis.

Since their meta-analysis, several new studies have added to our knowledge on this topic. Meglino, DeNisi, Youngblood and Williams (1988), in their study of U.S. Army trainees, found that subjects who received a traditional (reduction) preview had lower anticipated satisfaction on 3 of 5 satisfaction measures, suggesting that their expectations had indeed been lowered by the preview. Meglino, DeNisi and Ravlin (1993), in their study of corrections officer applicants, provided some additional support for the met expectations hypothesis by demonstrating that the RJP subjects expected more danger and injury on the job (i.e., had more realistic expectations) than did control group subjects. And Suszko and Breaugh (1986) found that RJP subjects were more satisfied with their jobs than non-RJP subjects, providing indirect support for the met expectations hypothesis.

Premack and Wanous found that commitment tended to be higher among new hires who had been exposed to RJPs, with a corrected mean correlation of .09. However, they found a small negative relationship between RJPs and perceptions of employer honesty. Thus their results support the general commitment effect, although it did not appear to operate through perceptions of honesty. More recently, however, Suszko and Breaugh (1986) found that RJP applicants did have higher perceptions of organizational honesty and openness than did control group applicants. Similarly, Meglino et al. (1988) found that applicants exposed to either a combined enhancement and reduction preview or a reduction preview alone saw the organization as more honest and trustworthy and more caring, and Meglino et al. (1993) also found that RJP recipients perceived the organization as more honest, trustworthy, and caring.

Premack and Wanous were unable to support the coping hypothesis based on their meta-analysis. They found a corrected mean correlation between exposure to realistic previews and coping (newcomers' perceived ability to handle job-related stress) of -0.01; this correlation is very small and also in the wrong direction. Consistent with this finding, Meglino et al. (1988) found that subjects exposed to a traditional (reduction) preview were more anxious than members of other groups about 3 of 15 job elements. However, Suszko and Breaugh (1986) found that RJP subjects had higher perceptions of their ability to cope with job demands than did control group subjects.

Self-Selection Versus Attraction:
RJPs and Immediate Recruitment Outcomes

The self-selection mechanism is particularly important to understanding RJPs' impact on recruitment. As Wanous and Colella (1989) pointed out, self-selection and organizational attraction are not synonymous. Self-selection refers to rejection of a job opportunity *because it is inconsistent with one's preferences and needs,* not merely because it is less attractive than some other offer. Yet, it is certainly possible that RJPs make jobs less attractive to *all* applicants, regardless of their personal need structures. This is particularly likely to happen when other jobs are (credibly) portrayed in more uniformly positive terms.

Empirical Research on Self-Selection

Reviews of RJP research often focus exclusively on field studies, as turnover effects are difficult to study in laboratory environments. In their meta-analytic review of such studies, Premack and Wanous (1985) found support for the self-selection hypothesis in that exposure to an RJP was associated with higher job rejection rates. A corrected mean correlation of .06 was observed; however, this result was only obtained after dropping one outlier study. Two later field studies find additional support for the effect. Suszko and Breaugh (1986) also found that applicants exposed to RJPs were more likely to turn down job offers than control group subjects. Meglino et al. (1993) found that applicants who had previous exposure to the job and who were exposed to a realistic preview were more likely to reject job offers.

Additional insight into the self-selection effect is provided by a series of studies by Saks and his colleagues (1990). Though these studies do not speak to turnover outcomes, they do contribute to our understanding of how RJPs might work, and place particular emphasis on self-selection effects.

Saks and Cronshaw (1990) conducted a lab study in which 60 undergraduate students participated in one of three employment interview simulations: one involving an oral RJP, one involving a written RJP, and a control condition in which only general information about the job was provided. Saks and Cronshaw found that job expectations were lower in preview groups, consistent with the met expectations hypothesis. In addition, they found partial support for the "air of honesty" hypothesis. What is most relevant to the present discussion is that they did not find evidence of self-selection. Neither form of RJP was associated with lower job acceptance intentions.

A shortcoming of the above study is that subjects were asked to respond to only one job alternative. As a result, subjects may have deemed the job "better than nothing" even when presented with realistic information. This shortcoming was remedied in Wiesner, Saks, and Summers (1991). This study, which focused on the self-selection hypothesis, involved 60 undergraduate students playing the role of applicants for a marketing job. Three experimental conditions were employed. Subjects reacted to: (1) a positive preview versus no job; (2) a realistic preview versus no job; or (3) a positive preview versus a negative preview versus no job. Attraction to the job and intended acceptance of the job did not differ across subjects in the first and second conditions (i.e., those with only one job to consider). Applicants who chose between positive and realistic preview jobs, however, strongly preferred the job that had been portrayed in a uniformly positive manner. In other words, RJPs appeared to have a negative impact on attraction only when a viable alternative was available.

Saks, Wiesner and Summers (1994) replicated and refined the previous study. Using a similar role-playing scenario, they focused on subjects' reasons for rejecting jobs. As noted earlier, self-selection implies that applicants withdraw themselves from consideration for a job because they see the job as inconsistent with their needs and preferences. But most studies of the self-selection effect (including all of those reviewed above) treat any rejection of a job as indicative of self-selection. In Saks et al., 138 undergraduate business students responded to the same experimental stimuli and conditions used in Wiesner et al. In this case, however, subjects' work-related needs were also assessed. Once again, differences in job acceptance rates were found only in the two-job condition, and when offered a choice, subjects expressed strong preferences for the positive preview job. Further, the authors found evidence that applicants were making choices that matched their needs with their job expectations—in other words, a self-selection mechanism was operating.

Saks, Wiesner and Summers (1996) expanded this stream still further by incorporating a job attribute, compensation policy, in their experimental design. Rynes and Barber (1990) argued that the effects of RJPs are likely not independent of characteristics of the jobs being previewed, but research does not typically consider attributes and realism simultaneously. Saks et al. (1996) used the two-job preview methodology of Wiesner et al. (1991) and incorporated a manipulation of pay level (average versus high), anticipating that high compensation levels might offset negative attraction effects associated with the RJP. Results indicated that subjects preferred the traditional-preview job when compensation levels were higher than or equal to compensation levels associated with the RJP job. When the RJP job offered higher compensation than the traditional-preview job, however, no differences in attraction were observed.

Do RJPs Seriously Impede Attraction?

Given the centrality of applicant attraction as a recruitment goal, careful consideration of RJP effects on the ability of the organizations to attract qualified applicants is in order. Yet we know fairly little about this issue. Evidence from field studies generally suggests that applicants are slightly more likely to reject jobs when RJPs used. It is unclear, however, whether this negative attraction effect is a problem from an organizational standpoint. If those who withdrew from the hiring process were likely to have quit shortly after being hired, the organization is probably better off without them. Unfortunately, we do not really know why applicants reject RJP jobs as few studies (and no field studies) have explored this question. Therefore, we cannot be sure that organizations that use RJPs are not losing desirable applicants. More research focusing on when and why applicants reject RJP jobs is warranted. Such research should consider the role of employment alternatives in the rejection of RJP jobs, as work by Saks and colleagues suggests that availability of other jobs may be a key factor. Job availability can vary as a function of economic conditions, or as a function of individual qualifications. Either of these factors suggests that negative attraction consequences of RJPs may indeed be problematic, as they may be most likely to occur when jobs are hard to fill or among the most sought-after and best-qualified applicants.

Conclusion

Our understanding of whether and how recruitment activities maintain applicant's interest and involvement throughout the selection process is perhaps best characterized as imbalanced. A large number of studies focus on applicant reactions to the initial interview (most frequently, the campus interview). This research suggests that applicants are influenced by initial interview experiences, at least in the short run, and that this influence to an extent exists because interviewers and interviews are used as signals of job or organizational characteristics. The practical value of this knowledge, however, depends on the extent to which these reactions are converted into behavioral responses such as rejecting a job offer or dropping out of the selection process (e.g., refusing a second interview) because of initial interview experiences, questions we know relatively little about.

There is a great need for research focusing on recruitment events subsequent to the initial interview (e.g., administrative procedures, site visits). These interactions are likely to have stronger impacts than the campus interview because they are longer in duration, involve contact with more than one organizational representative, and occur closer to the point of job choice. Recent research on applicant reactions to selection procedures represents a significant contribution to our understanding of how these later events influence applicant attraction.

Little attention has been paid to spillover effects associated with this stage of recruitment. A few studies have found spillover effects associated with applicant reactions to selection procedures (Macan, et al., 1994; Smither, et al., 1993), but spillover associated with campus recruitment has not been explored. This is surprising given that student grapevines are likely to spread information about positive and negative recruitment experiences rather rapidly. Overall, though the public relations aspects of recruitment (and interviews in particular) have been acknowledged, they have rarely been researched, and there is room for additional work on this topic.

Finally, recruitment realism remains one of the most thoroughly and systematically studied areas of recruitment. This work, however, has paid substantially more attention to post-hire outcomes (specifically, turnover) than to more immediate recruitment objectives (specifically, attraction effects). Though turnover can be a serious problem for organizations, inability to fill positions can also be problematic, and research balancing these two objectives is warranted.

4 Influencing Job Choice

This chapter deals with the final stage of the recruitment process: the stage during which applicants decide whether to accept job offers that they have received. The primary focus of existing research at this stage is on the applicant, and rightly so. Understanding the content and processes of applicant decision making is critical, as in aggregate those individual decisions determine how effectively and efficiently the organization's positions get filled. However, applicants do not make their decisions in a vacuum. Organizations can still be actively engaged in recruitment at this stage, and that is why this chapter is labeled "influencing job choice."

In this chapter, we first focus on the *content* of job acceptance decisions, that is, on the factors that appear to influence job acceptance. This discussion includes a debate over the relative importance of recruitment vis-à-vis job attributes in job choice. Next, we turn to the *processes* by which job acceptance decisions are made, examining how information about relevant factors is actually used in formulating a decision. Finally, we review how the circumstances surrounding job choice might affect post-hire outcomes.

A note of clarification is necessary before moving forward: This chapter addresses ultimate job choice decisions, that is, decisions regarding whether to accept or reject a job offer rather than decisions to pursue or not pursue employment through application and screening. I exclude studies of decisions that occur earlier in process, although those too can be construed as part of job choice (in that a job can certainly be rejected earlier on). Early decisions (reviewed in Chapter 2) are different in nature from later decisions. Early job choice decisions, such as the decision to apply, do not require the applicant to forego all other possibilities. They lead to a reduced set of opportunities but do not require the commitment to a single opportunity that is required in final job choice. Failure to differentiate these types of decisions may obscure decision content, process, or both. Some writers use the term *job offer acceptance* rather than *job choice* to more precisely identify the type of job choice examined in this chapter. However, the most common use of the term *job choice* is to refer to this final stage of choice, a convention that is followed here.

Thus this chapter focuses on what we know about (1) hypothetical and/or intended job choice and (2) actual job choice. As the following review will indicate, far more studies assess the former than the latter. However, recent evidence regarding the association of job choice intentions and actual job choice decisions is encouraging: Turban, Campion and Eyring (1995) found that intention to accept and actual acceptance decision were positively correlated (r =.50 and .53 for two separate samples), and that intentions and actual acceptance were predicted by same factors. Similarly, Cable and Judge (1996) observed a correlation of .48 between choice intentions and actual choice, and also found that variables used to predict choice intentions also predicted choice. Finally, Powell and Goulet (1996) found a correlation of .56 between post-interview intentions to accept a job and actual job acceptance. Therefore it appears that job acceptance intentions serve as a reasonable proxy for actual job choice.

Content Issues in Job Choice Decisions

Behling, Labovitz, and Gainer (1968) identified three "implicit theories" of job (position) choice: objective factors, subjective factors, and the critical contact approach. The objective factors perspective assumes that job choice decisions are based on weighing the advantages and disadvantages of objectively measurable job attributes, such as pay, working conditions, or nature of work. Job attributes are evaluated in terms of attractiveness and importance, and these evaluations are combined to form an overall assessment of the job's desirability. The subjective factors approach assumes that choice is based on perceived congruence between the individual and the firm with respect to subjective assessments of personality, needs, or values. This perspective suggests that applicants are most likely to choose positions with firms that they believe can meet their psychological needs. Finally, the critical contact perspective suggests that job seekers are often unable to make meaningful distinctions between the jobs in their decision set in terms of either objective or subjective factors, and therefore must rely on recruitment contacts as the only available means of differentiating among firms. Over the 30 years since Behling et al. wrote their article, most studies of the content of job choice have followed one of these three perspectives.

Objective Factors: The Role of Job Attributes

Early job choice research focused on the relative importance of different job characteristics. A typical approach was to provide research subjects with lists of job factors (e.g., pay, opportunities for advancement, nature of work) and ask them to either rate or rank the factors with respect to their importance. This approach has been called the "direct estimation" technique (Schwab, et al., 1987). Two of these studies are particularly noteworthy because of the extensive samples involved. Jurgensen (1978) provided data drawn from almost 57,000 individuals collected over a period of 30 years. His subjects were asked to rank the importance of 10 job attributes in terms of (1) their own personal preferences, and (2) what they perceived the preferences of others to be. Attributes included were advancement, benefits, company, coworkers, hours, pay, security, supervisor, and type of work. Personal preference rankings were remarkably similar over time and across demographic groups, although some gender differences were observed: Men tended to rank security as most important, whereas women tended to rank type of work as most important. Both men and women ranked pay near the middle of the 10 attributes when expressing their own preferences but felt that others would rank pay significantly higher than they themselves did. Turban, et al. (1993) recently applied Jurgensen's instrument to a sample of 110 applicants to a large chemical company and found that results were largely consistent with those reported by Jurgensen 15 years earlier. Turban et al., however, did not find significant gender differences.

In a second large-scale study, Lacy, Bokemeier and Shepard (1983) used data from five national surveys conducted between 1973 and 1980; a total of 7,281 respondents participated. They asked respondents to rank the following five attributes in order of importance: income, security, working hours, chances for advancement, and meaningfulness of work. They concluded that both men and women placed the greatest importance on having work that was meaningful, and that income and promotion were the second most important attributes.

Assessing the consistency of these results is difficult because the studies do not include equal numbers of attributes. For instance, Jurgensen (1978) and Lacy et al. (1983) have five attributes in common, and are therefore somewhat comparable. However, one cannot directly compare rankings because different numbers of attributes were used. A ranking of "1" would have the same meaning in both studies (i.e., it would indicate the most important attribute), whereas a ranking of "5" would mean the attribute was moderately important in the Jurgensen study (which included 10 attributes) but only minimally important in the Lacy et al. study (which included only 5).

It is possible, however, to compare rank orders within the set of attributes included in both studies. Table 4.1 presents three sets of rankings: Jurgensen's (1978) ratings of importance to self and importance to others, and Lacy et al.'s (1983) ratings of importance to self. (Results for men and women, presented separately in the original studies, were pooled for this comparison.) This table indicates that results were only partially consistent across these two large-sample studies. A comparison of the first and third columns indicates that respondents agreed that type of work was the most important attribute for themselves personally, and that hours of work were not particularly important. However, security was ranked as more important than advancement or pay by Jurgensen's subjects, whereas pay was viewed as more important than advancement or security by Lacy et al.'s subjects. The middle column also provides an interesting perspective: When asked which attributes *others* would consider important, Jurgensen's subjects ranked pay as the most important attribute and type

Table 4.1   Comparisons of rank orders: Jurgensen (1978) vs. Lacy et al. (1983)

	Jurgensen: Self	Jurgensen: Others	Lacy et al.
Type of work	1	4	1
Security	2	3	4
Advancement	3	2	3
Company	4	8	
Pay	5	1	2
Coworkers	6	10	
Supervision	7	9	
Benefits	8	6	
Hours	9	5	5
Working conditions	10	7	

of work as fourth in importance. These rankings are substantially different from those the subjects gave when providing their own personal views. Most commentators (e.g., Schwab, et al., 1987; Rynes, 1991) have attributed these differences to social desirability factors, suggesting that individuals are reluctant to express their true desire for high pay for fear of appearing greedy or overly materialistic.

Limitations of Direct Estimation

The direct estimation approach to assessing the importance of attributes in job choice suffers from a number of shortcomings. First, it is unclear whether preferences for job attributes necessarily translate into reliance on those attributes in job choice. As Schwab et al. (1987) noted, direct estimation studies do not explicitly link job attributes to job choice decisions; rather, it is assumed that the most preferred or most important attributes will have the most impact on job choice. Turban et al. (1993), in the study referred to above, provided evidence suggesting that this assumption may not be valid. They asked subjects to rank job attributes in terms of general importance and (in a second survey) importance in the decision to accept or reject a job offer. They found that the two rank orderings differed. For example, among those who rejected a job offer, location was ranked as the most important factor influencing their decision but ranked fourth in terms of general importance (behind type of work, opportunities for advancement, and coworkers). Interestingly, general importance and job choice importance were more highly correlated for applicants who accepted the job offer than for those who rejected the offer.

A second criticism of rating and ranking studies is that they are too abstract—they typically do not provide a context for respondents to use in assessing attribute importance. Two contextual elements are important: the relative levels of different attributes, and the amount of variation that exists for each attribute.

In actual job choice decisions, the relative importance of attributes likely depends on their levels and on the nature of the tradeoffs that might be made between them. Rottenberg (1956), in a classic paper on tradeoffs in job choice, provides the following example:

> Consider a worker with a given criteria system. If he rejects an offer of work in Greenland, he will explain his choice by saying, "It's too cold up there." If he accepts the offer, he will explain by saying, "They're paying good money." When he said, "It's too cold," what he really intended was, "It's too cold, for the money they're paying"; and, when he said, "They're paying good money," what he really intended was "They're paying good enough money, even for the cold that I will experience in Greenland." (p. 191)

As this example suggests, attributes are evaluated jointly, not separately. However, direct estimation studies typically provide little or no information about attribute levels and do not allow for joint evaluation, instead asking subjects to evaluate their importance in the abstract.

In addition, the importance of an attribute is likely dependent on its variability. Factors with little variation, although inherently important, cannot serve the purpose of discriminating among offers and therefore will not appear to be important determinants of choice. And, as Rynes et al. (1983) demonstrated, attributes that vary significantly across offers may receive more weight in job choice decisions than attributes that do not vary as much. Again, direct estimation studies do not provide subjects with an indication of how much the different attributes might vary across offers.

Third, direct estimation studies have been criticized as requiring (or expecting) too much self-insight on the part of subjects. The concern is that subjects may not actually know, or may be unable to articulate, the relative importance of various attributes in their decision-making. Thus they are not capable of providing accurate reports of attribute importance.

Policy-Capturing as an Alternative

Policy-capturing is an alternative approach to investigating the role of attributes in job choice that addresses some of the concerns associated with direct estimation. Under this approach, research subjects are presented with a series of job descriptions in which attribute levels are systematically varied. For each description, subjects are asked to indicate whether they would accept the job (or how likely they would be to accept the job). Subjects need not be asked to explicitly report the importance of specific attributes. Rather, regression analysis is used to calculate the relative impact the different attributes had on job choice. This approach has several advantages over direct estimation. It does not require self-insight on the part of applicants, it provides a context for the decision by providing information about attribute levels and variability, and it ties attribute variation directly to the job choice criterion.

An early example of this technique was provided by Feldman and Arnold (1978). They presented 62 graduate students with descriptions of job opportunities that provided information about the following attributes:

- opportunities to use one's skills and abilities
- amount of autonomy and independence
- responsibility
- providing essential services/products to the public
- salary and fringe benefits, and
- schedule flexibility.

Two levels of each attribute were used, with a completely crossed design resulting in 64 descriptions. Subjects read each description and indicated how willing they would be to accept the position described by marking a scale ranging from "extremely unwilling" to "extremely willing." Regression results indicated that salary and benefits explained the most variance in willingness to accept the job (in other words, that salary and benefits was the most important attribute), followed by use of skills and abilities, responsibility, autonomy, having flexible hours, and providing essential goods or services.

Feldman and Arnold (1978) also asked their subjects to rank order the importance of the six attributes included in their study. They then were able to compare direct estimation and policy-capturing results. The two sets of results did not agree. Most notably, pay, which was identified as the most important attribute by the policy-capturing analysis, was ranked by the subjects as fourth in importance (behind opportunity to use skills and abilities, autonomy, and responsibility). Other studies (e.g., Zedeck, 1977) have also found different results as a function of method employed.

While policy-capturing has some advantages over direct estimation techniques, it is by no means an ideal alternative. First, this approach generally requires subjects to evaluate a large number of jobs in a relatively short period of time. This creates an unrealistic decision-making scenario and raises concerns about subject fatigue and inattention (Breaugh, 1992). In addition, researchers' decisions about the amount of variability built into the design can influence results, and substantial care must be taken not to "stack the deck" in favor of certain attributes.

Finally, policy-capturing shares a weakness with direct estimation in that the attributes to be evaluated are chosen by the researcher rather than by the job applicant. This is an important issue, as failure to include attributes salient to job seekers could result in erroneous conclusions about the relative importance of specific attributes, or about the importance of job attributes in general as determinants of job choice. This problem is perhaps most severe with respect to policy-capturing, where the number of attributes considered is restricted (often to no more than five attributes) in order to ameliorate the subject fatigue concerns described above. Unfortunately, the decision rules by which some attributes are chosen for inclusion in research and others are excluded are not often clearly stated or justified.

One approach that can be used to avoid overlooking important attributes is to permit subjects to identify the attributes they considered. This approach was used in a job search study conducted by Barber, Daly, Giannantonio, and Phillips (1994). In this study, 186 college and vocational-technical school candidates were asked to list job and organizational characteristics they were considering in searching for jobs. Barber et al. then coded attributes into 27 categories, which were then subjected to further analysis.

A second approach to identifying important attributes would be to base selection of attributes on content-based theories of motivation. Surprisingly little of the job attribute research has taken advantages of existing categorizations to ensure that an appropriate range of attributes is considered, although Barber et al. (1994) and Wanous (1980, 1992) have used Alderfer's ERG model (Alderfer, 1969) as a means of classifying or identifying relevant attributes.

Demographic Differences
in Attribute Preferences

As noted earlier, lack of consistency in the attributes included in research makes it difficult to summarize findings regarding the importance of specific attributes in job choice. However, it is apparent that inconsistencies occur across studies. Several reasons for these discrepancies have already been suggested. Differences in method (e.g., direct estimation versus policy-capturing), frame of reference (e.g., own preferences versus supposed preferences of others), and attribute levels (e.g., amount of variation) can all influence conclusions about the relative importance of attributes. An additional explanation that has received significant research attention is that different types/groups of applicants may have different attribute preferences.

A number of researchers have posited that men and women have different job attribute preferences. For example, Jurgensen (1978) found evidence of such differences. In his study, men placed more importance on security than on type of work, but women viewed type of work as substantially more important than other factors. Similarly, Lacy et al. (1983) found that women held slightly stronger preferences for meaningful work, and men held slightly stronger preferences for security. However, more recent studies have failed to find gender differences, particularly when job level differences are controlled (e.g., Lefkowitz, 1994; Turban, et al., 1995; Wiersma, 1990). Barber and Daly (1996) suggested that the apparent reduction in gender differences over time may be due to reductions in the degree of sex role differentiation, gender discrimination, and occupational segregation that exists within society.

Other studies have explored relationships between work experience and attribute preferences, reasoning that preferences may change as one matures and/or becomes more knowledgeable about the world of work. Zedeck (1977) was able to identify four unique clusters of subjects who had relatively similar attribute preferences. Analyses of variance suggested the four groups differed in terms of age, work experience, organizational tenure, present salary, and marital status (effects of individual variables could not be clearly distinguished, as the factors were substantially intercorrelated). Zedeck's general conclusion was that older, more experienced subjects tended to place more emphasis on security, and younger, less experienced subjects attached more importance to pay. Feldman and Arnold (1978) found subjects with more work experience put more weight on responsibility and leadership and less on pay and fringe benefits than did subjects with less work experience. And Jurgensen (1978) found that young men attached more importance to pay (among other things) and less to security and advancement.

These three studies, then, are largely consistent in their findings. In particular, they suggest that the role of compensation likely changes with age and experience. On the other hand, Lacy et al. (1983) did not find age to be significantly related to attribute preference (they did not examine the role of work experience directly). Whether or not attribute preferences change with age and experience is an important question, given that much job choice research has used graduating college students as subjects. Evidence of age- related differences in attribute preferences calls into question the generalizability of that research. Therefore further research along these lines—and in particular research that provides theoretical rationale for age- and experience-based changes in preferences—is warranted.

Relatively few studies have examined relationships between psychological variables and attribute preferences per se. Feldman and Arnold (1978) found that growth need strength (GNS) was related to preferences: High GNS individuals attached more importance to being able to use their skills and on autonomy/independence, while low GNS individuals attached more importance to pay and benefits. Lacy et al. (1983) found that work commitment was negatively associated with preference for high income and short hours, and positively associated with preference for meaningful work. However, it is not the case that individual differences in needs, values, or personalities have been ignored in job choice research. Rather, research along these lines has generally been conducted under the rubric of Behling et al.'s (1968) second theory of job choice, the subjective factors or "fit" perspective.

Subjective Factors: "Fit"
Models of Job Choice

The second content-based approach to job choice described by Behling et al. (1968) was the subjective factors model. This model employs a matching or "fit" perspective. Its underlying logic is that individuals have different emotional and psychological needs and that they will seek jobs that best fit their individual needs. Similar logic has been employed in Tom's (1971) image model, Schneider's (1987) Attraction-Selection-Attrition (ASA) model, and Wanous's (1980, 1992) matching model.

In this instance, the "content" relied upon in job choice is subjective in nature and related to the applicant's needs. Beyond that, it is not entirely clear what factors are involved. For example, Tom (1971) matched individual *personalities* and *values* with perceived organizational image. Schneider (1987) did not explicitly identify the elements of fit, referring more generally to different "types" of individuals.

Wanous (1980, 1992) suggested that the critical elements of matching, from the applicants' perspective, are the applicants' basic *needs* (categorized using Alderfer's Existence-Relatedness-Growth model), which either are or are not consistent with the organization's culture.

Several studies have assessed the degree to which job choice can be predicted by examining congruence between individual and organizational characteristics, and interest in this topic has increased in recent years. In one of the earliest studies of fit in job choice, Tom (1971) had 100 college students who were looking for jobs evaluate both their most and their least preferred potential employers on two instruments: (1) the Adjective Check List, a 15-scale personality measure, and (2) the Study of Values, which assesses the prominence of six basic values: theoretical, economic, social, aesthetic, political, and religious. One week later, subjects completed the same scales with respect to themselves. Profile comparisons indicated that the most preferred organizations were significantly more similar to the individuals' self-evaluations than were the least preferred organizations, supporting the subjective congruence theory.

More recently, Bretz, Ash, and Dreher (1989) assessed whether congruence between internal need states and organizational environments was related to job choice. In this study, graduating college students viewed two videotapes: one depicting a company whose reward system was largely individually oriented, and one whose reward system was emphasized collective organizational outcomes. Bretz et al. predicted that subjects high in need for achievement (nACh) would prefer the individualistic reward system, whereas subjects high in need for affiliation (nAff) would prefer the organizationally oriented system. They found limited support for their hypotheses. No main effects were found for either nAch or nAff, although a significant interaction between the two was found. Post hoc analyses provided some additional support for the general congruence model. In these analyses, relationships between organizational choice and two higher-order personality traits were examined. High levels of orientation toward work, a more general trait that implies an orientation toward individual work accomplishment and includes nAch, were associated with preference for the organization with the individually oriented reward system. However, no significant relationship was found between organizational choice and quality of interpersonal orientation, a second-order trait that incorporates nAff.

Judge and Bretz (1992) examined the role of work value congruence in job choice. In this policy-capturing study, 67 undergraduate and graduate college students reviewed 128 job descriptions and were asked to indicate the likelihood that they would accept the described job. The descriptions varied in terms of objective job characteristics (pay, promotion opportunities, and type of work). They also included statements reflecting varying degrees of four central values: achievement, honesty, fairness, and concern for others. Congruence was assessed in a between-subjects analysis by examining interactions between subjects' own values and the values portrayed in the descriptions—likelihood of accepting the offer was expected to be highest when organizational and individual values were congruent. Results largely supported this hypothesis: congruence with respect to fairness, concern for others, achievement, and honesty was associated with higher probabilities of acceptance.

Bretz and Judge (1994) assessed whether job acceptance would be influenced by the degree to which human resource systems (e.g., reward and promotion systems) matched individual characteristics. Sixty-five graduate and undergraduate students viewed 128 job descriptions that varied in terms of reward system (individual vs. group), promotion system (contest vs. sponsored mobility), justice systems (mentioned vs. not mentioned) and work/family policies (mentioned or not mentioned). Salary level and promotional opportunities were also systematically varied. Subjects evaluated each description by indicating how likely they were to accept a job offer from the organization. Results supported the congruence model. Probability of accepting an offer was significantly associated with interactions between each of the human resource systems and associated individual characteristics.

Cable and Judge (1996; also Judge & Cable 1997) added considerably to the fit literature by conducting field studies of applicant perceptions of person-organization fit. In Cable and Judge (1996), 96 college student job seekers were surveyed at three points in time to assess perceptions of fit (defined in terms of values), job choice intentions, and post-hire outcomes, including organizational commitment, job satisfaction, and turnover intentions. They found that applicant perceptions of person-organization fit significantly predicted their job choice intentions, even after the attractiveness of job attributes was controlled. In addition, they found that applicants who perceived greater person-organization fit prior to being hired showed greater commitment, job satisfaction, willingness to recommend the organization to others, and lower turnover intentions than applicants with lower initial impressions of their own fit with the organization. Judge and Cable (1997) surveyed 182 college students who were seeking employment and found that both objective and subjective assessments of person-organization fit (with respect to values) were related to a measure of attraction to the organization. In addition, they showed that applicant attraction to organizations with specific types of cultures could be predicted on the basis of personality characteristics. However, in this study actual job choices were not associated with either objective or subjective measures of fit.

Overall, support for the subjective factors theory is fairly strong, but to date the research is limited by both conceptual and practical difficulties. On the conceptual side, studies have varied with respect to the kinds of factors that applicants will seek to match. As Judge and Cable (1997) described it, "(j)ob seekers' goals, values, needs, interests and personalities have been compared with organizations' cultures, pay systems, sizes, structures, and values" (p. 359). This difficulty in defining content is endemic to the person-environment fit literature in general (see Kristof, 1996). Chatman and colleagues (Chatman, 1989, 1991; O'Reilly, Chatman, & Caldwell, 1991) have argued that values are the central element of fit, as they are a "fundamental and enduring aspect of both organizations and people" (Chatman, 1989, p. 339). However, needs and personalities are also fundamental and enduring aspects of individuals, and it is difficult to argue that they would not influence job choice. In reality, all three are likely to matter, and research examining applicants' attempts to match on multiple aspects would present a more complete picture of the subjective factors process than would research focusing on only one element of matching. Indeed, Judge and Cable's finding that personality characteristics predict value preferences suggests that these dimensions of fit *must* be studied jointly if they are to be thoroughly understood.

Methodologically, matching or fit studies of job choice are limited by the fact that they have focused exclusively on college students. In addition, with few exceptions (Cable & Judge, 1996; Judge & Cable, 1997; Tom, 1971) these studies have used hypothetical companies and information about the companies has been closely controlled by the researcher. Expansion of this line of research into field settings should be applauded, and research involving experienced job seekers is strongly encouraged.

Critical Contact Perspective: The Role of Recruitment

A third stream of research on the content of job choice decisions stems from Behling et al.'s "critical contact" perspective. According to this model, job applicants typically lack the information required to make decisions based on either objective or subjective factors. Because they cannot differentiate among offers on these grounds, they must grasp at other, more distinctive information. Behling et al. (1968) suggested that various aspects of the recruitment process (e.g., characteristics of the recruiter, efficiency of the recruitment process) are used, in the absence of other information, as indicators of organizational climate. In short, this perspective suggests that recruitment influences job choice because it is all that is available to base judgments on. This perspective clearly is consistent with the signaling hypotheses underlying much of the existing recruitment research discussed in the preceding chapter.

The impact of recruitment practices on job choice has been reviewed extensively in Chapters 2 and 3. To summarize, evidence suggests that job choice (or, in many cases, intentions of accepting a job offer) is a function of reactions to recruiter characteristics, especially recruiter warmth (Alderfer & McCord, 1970; Harris & Fink, 1987; Maurer, et al., 1992; Powell 1991; Schmitt & Coyle, 1976; Taylor & Bergmann, 1987), although these effects have not been found universally (see Rynes & Miller, 1983, or Powell, 1984). In addition, there is some evidence that recruiters' demographic characteristics are related to likelihood of offer acceptance (Taylor & Bergmann, 1987) although this finding was not confirmed in other studies (e.g., Maurer, et al., 1992). Mixed results have been obtained regarding whether the nature of the interview influences job acceptance. For instance, Taylor and Bergmann (1987) found that interview structure was related to higher probabilities of job acceptance, but Turban and Dougherty (1992) concluded it had no effect. Little attention has been paid to recruitment processes and practices subsequent to interview, but there is some evidence that site visits can influence job choice (Rynes, 1991; Turban, et al. 1995), though not all studies concluded that the effect was significant (Taylor & Bergmann, 1987). Finally, the nature of information provided during recruitment (specifically, whether realistic job previews are employed) has been associated with reduced likelihood of offer acceptance (Premack & Wanous, 1985).

As noted in Chapter 1, recruitment is a series of activities, any one of which may influence an applicant's decision to pursue employment with an organization or to accept a job if one is offered. What is remarkable about recruitment research to date is the degree to which it focuses on the impact of one single recruitment event, the initial screening interview, as a potential influence on job choice. In fact, though two other aspects of recruitment—source of applicants and communication realism—have been extensively researched, these streams have focused only incidentally on attraction consequences (focusing instead on post-hire consequences). As a result, our understanding of whether and how recruitment influences job choice might be better characterized as an understanding of whether and how the initial interview influences job choice. We know little about the impact of events that occur earlier than the interview, such as whether initial images have influence that persists after the initial decision to apply has been made. Nor do we know a great deal about events that follow the initial screening interview but precede job offers, such as the site visit or reactions to selection procedures.

Furthermore, there is very little research investigating how recruitment practices that occur as or after an offer is extended influence job choice. Taylor and Bergmann (1987) found that a variable called "treatment during decision period" was significantly associated with perceptions of company attractiveness but was unrelated to job choice or to turnover intentions. The sample used for this analysis, however, was quite small, and failure to find effects may have been due to power limitations (particularly for turnover intentions, for which the observed effect size was reasonably large). The absence of additional research on these later events is particularly troubling, as it is likely that events occurring closer to the choice itself will be more salient and therefore will have more impact than events that occurred at earlier stages. For instance, Hogarth and Einhorn (1976) suggested that acceptance rates might be increased by making "on the spot" offers to desirable candidates. Such offers might be particularly effective with applicants who are eager to reduce the uncertainties associated with job search. In addition, policies regarding deadlines for accepting offers, start dates, and relocation expenses might significantly impact applicant attraction, either because they are important in their own right or because they are seen as symbolic of organizational values or practices. Finally, negotiations (if any) that take place during this phase may be critical indicators of organizational flexibility and also may be important in setting the tone for future exchanges. Until research investigating the impact of such practices on job choice decisions is conducted, we can say little about the impact of recruitment *as a whole* on job choice.[1]

Integrating Models of Job Choice Content

The preceding review of the literature pertaining to each of Behling et al.'s (1968) models of job choice content provides at least some support for each. It is perhaps a natural inclination to try to decide which model is the "better" representation of the content of job choice. Indeed, a stream of research labeled "the contest" by Wanous and Collela (1989) attempted to determine whether job attributes or recruitment practices had a greater impact on job choice (e.g., Harris & Fink, 1987; Powell, 1984, 1991; Taylor & Bergmann, 1987).

Such contests are unlikely to be very fruitful for several reasons. First, it is extremely difficult to set up a fair test of the relative importance of the different elements (Cooper & Richardson, 1986). Fairness would require that, for each model, the most important components are included. For example, it would be unfair to pit the importance of a single job attribute against the full spectrum of recruitment practices, just as it would be unfair to compare the influence of a comprehensive list of job attributes to the effect of a single aspect of recruitment, such as recruiter behaviors, or a single aspect of matching, such as on values but not on personality or needs. The data collection requirements associated with attempts to assess all relevant dimensions of the three models are a bit mind-boggling. Furthermore, we cannot say with confidence at this point what exactly the relevant dimensions of each model are!

Second, Behling et al.'s (1968) models are not mutually exclusive. Therefore, there is no real need to identify *the* correct model—in all probability, each is correct to a degree. In fact, the models may be rather difficult to disentangle. For example, recruitment practices and objective job factors may both serve as the bases of inferences about an organization's values or ability to meet needs. (It is hard to imagine how applicants would determine whether or not a match exists if they were not to rely on either recruitment practices or job attributes.) As another example, salary negotiations that take place during the recruitment process may be important as indicators of the organization's flexibility and willingness to accommodate employee needs. They may also, however, result in higher starting salaries. Whether the impact of such negotiations should be attributed to reactions to recruitment procedures or reactions to attributes is unclear. It seems more appropriate, given evidence of the validity of all three models, to accept that they all matter to a degree and begin to study the interplay among them. This approach has been taken, at least indirectly, by several researchers. For instance, Harris and Fink (1987) examined whether recruiters changed applicant beliefs about job attributes, and Bretz and colleagues (e.g., Bretz, et al., 1989) have used observed job attributes as indicators of subjective job factors.

Above concerns about the difficulties of comparing these models notwithstanding, such comparisons might have practical value to organizations, but only if comparisons go beyond assessing relative influence on applicants. The practical value of any of these models, from the organizational standpoint, is a function of both whether they can influence applicant choice and how easily they can be modified. For instance, if recruitment practices can be easily (and inexpensively) changed whereas important job attributes are more difficult to change, organizations might choose to focus on recruitment as a means of increasing applicant attraction, even if attributes were, overall, "more important" (Rynes & Barber, 1990).Thus research addressing the relative utility of these three approaches to influencing job choice is warranted.[2]

In addition, future research might consider these three theories of job choice from a prescriptive point of view. To date, most research has focused on determining how job choices *are* made, rather than on how they *should* be made. However, Cable and Judge's (1996) findings that pre-hire perceptions of person-organization fit were associated with positive post-hire consequences suggest that it may be appropriate to counsel job seekers to evaluate prospective employers in terms of fit—in other words, to prescribe the subjective factors model as one that should be employed.

Job Choice Process

The process perspective on job choice focuses on *how* information is used in deciding to accept or reject a job offer rather than on *what* information is used. Far and away the most popular approach to examining the job choice process involves "expected value" models, a general class of decision-making models that presume decisions are based on the probability of obtaining certain outcomes multiplied by the value or attractiveness of those outcomes (Mitchell & Beach, 1976). This general class of theories includes expectancy theory, decision theory, and subjective utility theories. Of those, the best known and most used within the job choice literature is expectancy theory. In the sections that follow, the expectancy approach to job choice and empirical evidence supporting it are reviewed. Limitations of this approach, along with alternative views of how jobs are chosen, are then discussed.

Expectancy Models of Job Choice

Expectancy theory (Vroom, 1964) actually encompasses two models: one assessing the attractiveness of an outcome (in this scenario, a particular job), and one assessing motivation to exert effort toward achieving that outcome. The attractiveness (or valence) model states that individuals will assess the attractiveness of a job based on the attractiveness of job or organizational characteristics (i.e., valence, or *V*) and the likelihood that those characteristics will be present in the job (i.e., instrumentality, or *I*). The attractiveness of each attribute is multiplied by its instrumentality, and those products are summed to yield an overall attractiveness score, which can be expressed algebraically as:

$$(4.1) \qquad \text{Attractiveness} = \Sigma\,(V^*I)$$

The motivation model expands on the attraction model by arguing that individuals will exert the most effort toward options that maximize the product of the attractiveness score and the person's perceived probability that his or her effort will lead to the desired outcome (in this case, receipt of a job offer). This latter term is known as expectancy (*E*). Thus the motivation model can be portrayed as:

$$(4.2) \qquad \text{Force to perform (exert effort)} = E \times \Sigma(V^*I)$$

In the present context, we presume that applicants are choosing from among job offers that have already been received. Therefore the attractiveness model is most relevant. Expectancy in this case is 1.0; thus, its inclusion adds nothing to the model. In addition, there is little "effort" left to be exerted once the job offer has been received. This is in contrast to earlier job choice decisions, in which the more complete model was relevant (see Chapter 2).

Many studies have assessed the appropriateness/predictive validity of expectancy models in explaining the job choice process. For instance, Vroom (1966) had 49 graduating students complete surveys identifying the relative importance of 15 goals (e.g., chance to learn new things, stable and secure future) and the likelihood that each of these values could be obtained in a set of three organizations with which he (all subjects were male) was pursuing employment. These measures assessed valence and instrumentality of outcomes, respectively, and were combined in accordance with the above formula to yield an overall attractiveness score. Subjects were also asked to rank order and rate the attractiveness of the three jobs. Results indicated strong relationships between attractiveness scores derived from the expectancy formula and subjective assessments of attractiveness. In addition, attractiveness scores were effective in predicting actual job choice (among those who received offers from their most attractive organization).

Several reviews of the use of expectancy theory to predict job choice have been published (e.g., Wanous, 1977; Wanous, Keon, & Latack, 1983), and the general conclusion is positive: Expectancy models do seem to predict both attraction to organizations and actual organizational choice. Nonetheless, there are many who argue that expectancy models are not an accurate reflection of the job choice process. Expectancy models rest on several assumptions that have been questioned in the context of job choice. First, they presume that job choice is highly rational—that job seekers consider and weigh information on a reasonably large number of job-related factors. Second, they assume that information on these various factors is treated in a compensatory fashion—that attractive levels on one factor can compensate for unattractive levels on another. Third, they imply that job seekers simultaneously consider a number of alternatives, choosing from that set the job that offers the highest probability of providing desired attributes. Objections to each of these assumptions are described below.

Alternative Views of Job Choice

How Rational is Job Choice?

One of the better known alternatives to expectancy-based models of job choice is Soelberg's Generalizable Decision Processing (GDP) model, also known as decision confirmation theory (Power & Aldag, 1985) Soelberg (1967) argued that the "mathematical elegance" of utili   sed decision models was a poor representation of actual dec..   making processes. He proposed that Simon's (1947) model of limited rationality provided a better starting point for developing a theory of job choice. The limited rationality perspective suggests that job choice decisions will be based on satisficing strategies: Job seekers will choose the first job that meets minimum requirements on a few criteria rather than continuing to search for a job that will optimize all criteria. With this as a foundation, Soelberg interviewed 20 business school graduates repeatedly over 3- to 5-month periods regarding their job search and choice processes. Content analyses of these interviews led to a model of job choice in which job seekers do not use elaborate mathematical choice models, at least not before job choices are made. Rather, they identify "implicit favorites" based only on 1 or 2 primary attributes. These initial choices are not immediately made public, however. Before they can be announced, job searchers engage in a choice confirmation process, during which they develop a rationale to support their initial choice. It is at this point that elaborate decision models may be used. According to Soelberg, however, their use is primarily an "exercise in prejudice," (Soelberg, 1967, p. 26) in that evaluations and weighting of factors are distorted *post hoc* to ensure that the implicit favorite emerged as the "rational" choice.

Soelberg's model is less rational than expectancy models in several ways. First, it suggests that job seekers base decisions on fairly little information. Furthermore, it suggests that what might appear to be comprehensive evaluation processes are really no more than exercises in rationalization. In addition, though Soelberg provides little guidance as to how implicit favorites are initially chosen, it is certainly possible that such choices are made on the basis of emotional or intuitive reactions rather than on objective criteria.

As Power and Aldag (1985) noted in their review of Soelberg's model, there have been few empirical attempts to confirm Soelberg's theory, and many of them suffered from methodological shortcomings. For instance, Glueck (1974) classified job seekers as "satisficers" if they accepted the first and only offer received, "validators" if they accepted the first offer received but only after acquiring a second offer, and "maximizers" if they considered more than two alternatives. Glueck argued that Soelberg's theory requires most job searchers to be validators, and interpreted his findings that relatively few were validators as failure to support the GDP model. As Power and Aldag (1985) noted, however, it is not at all clear from Soelberg's work that his theory requires job searchers to consider two and only two alternatives.

Sheridan, Richards and Slocum (1975) conducted a study that compared expectancy theory with Soelberg's theory. Sheridan et al. studied 49 nursing school graduates as they looked for jobs, assessing whether they made implicit initial choices, whether those choices were made on the basis of many or few characteristics, and whether evaluations of job attractiveness changed after initial choices were made. Their findings provided mixed support for Soelberg's model. Consistent with Soelberg's theory, subjects typically did identify early favorites, and most often accepted jobs with their early favorites. In addition, many subjects reported that they continued to search after choosing an early favorite so that they would have comparison candidates. But evidence did not support the argument that initial favorites were chosen on the basis of few, rather than many, attributes. Furthermore, there was no evidence that subjects distorted their impressions of the attractiveness of alternative jobs after initial favorites were selected.

I was unable to locate any research on Soelberg's model conducted subsequent to Power and Aldag's (1985) review. This is not terribly surprising, given that the model is inherently difficult to test. A full and complete test would require researchers to document implicit choices prior to the point at which applicants are willing to admit that they have *made* implicit choices, presenting data collection problems that are hard to overcome. Nonetheless, the model does provide an intriguing counterpoint to the more rational expectancy-based approach, and has a number of implications that may be more amenable to testing than the model itself. For example, the choice confirmation stage, an important component of Soelberg's model, serves a variety of purposes: It allows job seekers time to verify information about their implicit choice, to negotiate improvements in the initial offer, to develop rationale for accepting the offer, and to ensure that better offers are not forthcoming (Power & Aldag, 1985). All of this suggests that the confirmation phase may be critical to post-hire outcomes, such as commitment to, and satisfaction with, the job/organization that was chosen. Therefore one way to examine the importance of this phase would be to investigate whether applicants for whom this phase is truncated experience lower post-hire commitment and satisfaction than those who are able to complete this phase. Such truncation might occur, for example, when an applicant is required to make a decision regarding one offer before alternative offers can be generated.

Is Job Choice Compensatory or Noncompensatory?

Expectancy theory is a compensatory decision model in that low instrumentalities or valences for certain attributes can be offset by high instrumentalities or valences for other attributes. The multiplicative nature of the model allows for such trade-offs. An alternative argument, however, suggests that job choice decision making may instead be noncompensatory.

Decision-making theory suggests that *choice* (selection of a single alternative) as opposed to *judgment* (evaluation of one or many alternatives) is likely to be characterized by noncompensatory processes (Billings & Sherer, 1988; Einhorn, Kleinmuntz, & Kleinmuntz, 1979). Choice in its essence is a process of ruling out alternatives, an objective efficiently accomplished via noncompensatory approaches, such as elimination by aspects (Tversky, 1972). This view is consistent with Simon's (1947) model of limited rationality in decision making. Because the decision to accept a job is a choice rather than a judgment, application of decision-making theory leads to an argument that job choice is likely to be noncompensatory. Along these lines, it should be noted that economic models of job choice have traditionally taken a noncompensatory view in suggesting that jobs are accepted or rejected on the basis of a reservation (or minimally acceptable) wage (Reynolds, 1951; Lippman & McCall, 1976).

A few studies have provided evidence that noncompensatory decision models may be used in job choice. For instance, Sheridan, Richards and Slocum (1975) and Turban et al. (1993), though not explicitly testing whether compensatory or noncompensatory models were used, found evidence consistent with noncompensatory decision making. Both studies found that applicants tended to reject job offers based on location, regardless of other characteristics.

The question of compensatory versus noncompensatory job choice models was studied directly by Osborn (1990). Osborn surveyed 96 college-level job seekers at three points in time. He assessed (1) whether they held minimum (or "special") requirements regarding geographic location, size of city or town, salary, and type of work; (2) their perceptions of the attractiveness/ importance of those four attributes in their job choice decision; (3) their perceptions of the likelihood that specific (actual) jobs would provide desirable levels of those four attributes and (4) their intended job choice. Osborn found that most (88.5%) of the subjects reported some minimum or special requirements that had to be met in order for them to consider a job, and that subjects' ratings of job acceptability were generally consistent with their asserted requirements. In general, most jobs that failed to meet stated criteria were rated as unacceptable, and most jobs that met stated criteria were rated acceptable. Osborn also constructed an index of attractiveness based on the expectancy formulation (i.e., ΣV^*I) by summing products of the attractiveness of, and likelihood of obtaining, the four attributes. Interestingly, he found that acceptability ratings often violated the predictions of expectancy theory in that jobs that were rated unacceptable sometimes had higher scores on the $\Sigma V^* I$ index than jobs that were rated acceptable.

It should be noted, however, that in no case have studies found the use of noncompensatory models to be universal. Instead, it seems that some job seekers use compensatory models and others use noncompensatory models. This suggests that we need to learn more about *when* the different models might be used rather than *whether* they are used.

Are Job Choice Decisions Made Simultaneously or Sequentially?

In the context of job choice, simultaneous decision making occurs when job seekers accumulate a number of job offers and then decide which offer to choose from the existing set. Sequential job choice occurs when job seekers evaluate offers one at a time, in each case making a decision either to accept a particular offer or to reject it and continue searching. Though expectancy theory can be applied to either kind of choice, in practice studies of expectancy models of job choice have taken a simultaneous decision-making perspective. What is typically studied is the process by which job seekers choose from among a variety of jobs.

It is unclear, however, whether many—or most—job seekers engage in simultaneous evaluation of multiple offers. Recent (or soon-to-be) college graduates seem more likely than most to be in a position to accumulate a pool of offers. Employers are aware that college graduates enter the market on a fixed cycle, and tend to time their recruitment efforts to match the employees' availability. This means that a host of employers will be extending offers during a well-defined time period, increasing the likelihood that any given individual will be able to obtain and assess multiple offers. Of course, not all college graduates will be fortunate enough to have multiple offers, particularly when the economy is weak. In addition, job seekers in other markets (in particular, experienced hires) do not face such well-defined hiring cycles and may not be able to accumulate a pool of offers before being required to make a decision. In cases such as these, the only "choice" that can be made is whether to accept a single offer or keep searching.

Research has not yet addressed whether or when job searchers accumulate multiple offers before making decisions. Blau (1992), in a study of the job search activities of 8,098 employed and unemployed job searchers, found that receipt of multiple offers was common. Many job searchers rejected at least one offer before accepting a job, but it is unclear from his study whether these rejections imply sequential or simultaneous choice.

The question is an important one, as there is reason to believe that whether decisions are sequentially or simultaneously made has implications for the decision that is made. Bazerman, Schroth, Shah, Diekmann, and Tenbrunsel (1994) examined the effect of single (sequential) versus multiple (simultaneous) offers on the job choice decision making of MBA students. In hypothetical job choice exercises, subjects with only one offer to "choose" (i.e., accept or reject) were more strongly influenced by social information, that is, information about the outcomes of others that had no bearing on the objective outcomes of the decision maker, than were subjects who chose from among several offers. Apparently, external referents were used when internal comparisons were not available. What is particularly interesting is that this study demonstrated that job preferences may actually shift, depending on whether the decision maker was faced with simultaneous or sequential decisions.

Soelberg's (1967) model suggests that sequential job choice may result in problems in later adjustment to the job. The confirmation phase is a critical part of his model. Soelberg argued that job seekers are unwilling to commit to a choice until they have at least one alternative against which to compare it. Sequential search, however, rules out that sort of comparison. To the extent that confirmation reduces concerns or anxieties about the job that is chosen, the absence of confirmation may well lead to lower satisfaction or commitment after the applicant is hired.

This literature suggests that whether job choices are made simultaneously or sequentially can have implications for individuals as well as for organizations. It can effect the nature of the decision that is made, as well as affective reactions to that decision, which in turn may be related to behavioral outcomes. It is possible that simultaneous job choice results in "better" decisions both for organizations and for applicants, an issue that merits investigation because of its practical implications. If simultaneous decision making leads to more objective decision making (Bazerman, et al., 1994) or higher initial commitment to the chosen job (Soelberg, 1967), it might behoove employers and employment intermediaries (e.g., search firms, hiring agencies) to facilitate simultaneous choice to the extent that it is not currently available.

Why Have Expectancy Models Been
Successful in Predicting Job Choice?

The preceding sections indicate a number of areas in which expectancy theory, as typically applied to job choice, may be an inadequate representation of how decisions are made. Yet the fact remains that expectancy models have successfully predicted job choice in a number of instances. An appropriate question, then, is how or why this "inappropriate" model can achieve such promising results. There are at least two explanations: one dealing with the methods used to study job choice research, and one dealing with the nature of job choice.

First, one must note that virtually all empirical tests of expectancy theory have been conducted in college placement settings. It can be argued that these settings are more likely than others to generate findings supportive of expectancy theory. As noted earlier, graduating college students are more likely than other job seekers to have a pool of offers from which to choose. They are also more likely than less educated job seekers to be able to engage in the fairly intricate weighting of information required by the expectancy model. Second, most tests of expectancy theory have employed policy-capturing and hypothetical scenarios. As Billings and Sherer (1988) noted, policy-capturing requires judgment rather than choice and therefore may result in more compensatory processes than would be used in a choice setting. Furthermore, as Osborn (1990) argued, tightly controlled laboratory settings may have the side effect of reducing the amount of information job seekers have to manage, again tipping the balance toward compensatory models. In short, it may be that the positive findings of expectancy studies of job choice are at least in part an artifact of their design.

Alternatively, it may be that expectancy theory provides a reasonable and useful explanation of *some* aspects of job choice for *some* individuals. As noted earlier, graduating college students may be more likely to use expected-value type models in making job choices than others. This merely suggests that the results of existing research will not generalize—it does not invalidate findings with respect to college graduates. Furthermore, expectancy theory may be relevant at selected moments during the choice decision. Osborn (1990) argued that applicants will use noncompensatory strategies early in job choice to narrow the pool of potential employers. He stated that the relevant criteria will at that point shift (because jobs not meeting the primary criteria will have been eliminated from the pool). It is possible that, following this initial screening, the nature of the decision process also changes from a noncompensatory approach to a compensatory approach more consistent with expectancy theory.

What is needed at this stage is a more inclusive approach to job choice models, one that is sensitive to contingency factors, such as shifts in decision-making strategies over time or differences in decision-making modes across labor markets or across individuals. An advantage of such research is that it would simultaneously contribute to our understanding of not only job choice but also decision making in general. In addition, use of more varied subject pools (e.g., more attention to the job choice processes of experienced employees) and more varied research techniques (e.g., use of process tracing techniques) in empirical tests of job choice would lead to a more fully rounded understanding of the job choice process.

Job Choice Processes
and Post-Hire Outcomes

Job choice has an obvious connection to post-hire work attitudes and behaviors. Job choice determines the characteristics of one's job and one's employer, and these job and organizational characteristics in turn are important determinants of one's experience with and reactions to work. The job choice process, however, also has more subtle implications for post-hire outcomes in that the act of choosing a job may trigger psychological mechanisms that in turn influence post-hire attitudes.

First, the job choice process might in itself alter employees' views of the attractiveness of the organization they have chosen to work for. One of the most notable contributions of Soelberg's job choice model is its focus on the confirmation phase. During this phase, job seekers reconcile themselves to the choice they are about to make. They resolve uncertainties associated with the decision, and may perceptually distort information about the job chosen (as well as those rejected) in order to develop an unambiguous rationale for their choice (Soelberg, 1967). In short, the fact of having chosen a job may cause changes in how that job is evaluated.

Though Soelberg (1967) was the first to explicitly incorporate a confirmation phase as part of the choice model, he was not the first to recognize that job seekers might adjust their perceptions of job attributes and attractiveness in order to rationalize their choice. Vroom

(1966) suggested the same general argument, although he suggested that perceptual distortion would occur subsequent to job choice. Vroom based his argument on cognitive dissonance theory (Festinger, 1957). According to this theory, uncertainties about the appropriateness of one's choice create a tension that decision makers reduce by reevaluating the option chosen (by inflating its attractiveness) and the option(s) not chosen (by deflating their attractiveness). Vroom studied the job choices of 49 business school graduates, measuring their assessments of job opportunities both prior to and after job choice. Consistent with his hypothesis, he concluded that attractiveness differentials between chosen and unchosen jobs increased subsequent to choice: Subjects generally rated their chosen job as the most attractive opportunity both before and after choice, but the gap between the chosen and unchosen jobs was larger following choice. Additional analyses suggested that this reevaluation occurred primarily through the de-valuation of jobs that were rejected.

Lawler, Kuleck, Rhode, and Sorenson (1975) provided additional evidence of a dissonance reduction effect. They studied the job choices and post-decision attitudes of 431 accounting students from 24 different universities. Subjects evaluated the attractiveness of a set of large public accounting firms prior to applying, after choosing a job, and again after one year of employment. Data collected immediately after job choice supported predictions based on dissonance theory: Chosen firms were rated as more attractive after choice than before, and rejected firms were rated as less attractive after choice than before. One year later, ratings of rejected firms were lower than ever, and ratings of chosen firms had fallen somewhat from their immediate post-choice level but remained higher than they had been prior to choice.

A second psychological mechanism that may be triggered by the job choice process itself involves reactions to the degree of volition job seekers have in making their choice. For example, O'Reilly and Caldwell (1980) hypothesized that job choices made in the presence of external constraints (e.g., financial pressures, family pressures) would result in lower satisfaction with, and commitment to, the new job than choices occurring under greater freedom of choice. O'Reilly and Caldwell surveyed 101 MBA graduates immediately prior to their graduation and again 6 months later. Their results suggested that external decision constraints were associated with lower subsequent satisfaction and commitment, but it is unclear to what extent these reactions are due to lack of volition per se. An alternative view is that external constraints forced some applicants to choose jobs that were inherently less attractive, and that negative post-hire outcomes stem from objective characteristics of the job chosen rather than of the choice process itself. Additional research is needed to clarify this issue.

Taken as a whole, this research suggests that the relationship between job choice processes and post-hire outcomes may be quite rich and could be a fruitful area for future research. In addition to helping us understand how employees adjust to job choices and to new work environments, such research could also have substantial practical implications. For example, vocational counselors might be able to "inoculate" job searchers against negative reactions associated with restricted job choice. These subtle relationships between job choice and later reactions to work also have methodological implications, in that they suggest that retrospective reports of why jobs were chosen are likely to be inaccurate representations of how jobs are evaluated at the time of choice.

Conclusion

A significant body of literature has focused on how applicants choose jobs. Both the content and the process on which job choice decisions are based have been examined. The relationship of job choice to recruitment is clear: A primary objective of recruitment is to attract prospective employees, and job choice provides a clear and tangible measure of whether attraction has succeeded.

Recruitment, however, is only one of many factors that might influence job choice, and job choice research has, appropriately, considered a wide range of determinants. The extent to which recruitment influences job choice is difficult to determine, for reasons described above. Yet the best evidence suggests that it carries weight. Interestingly, there is very little research on how recruitment activities that occur as applicants are making job choices (e.g., offer procedures, negotiations) might influence those choices, and additional knowledge about these potential effects is badly needed.

In addition, we need to know more about how job choice, and the circumstances under which job choices are made, influences post-hire consequences, such as satisfaction, turnover, and commitment. Most of what we know about recruitment's influences on these post-hire outcomes stems from recruitment activities that occur fairly early in the recruitment process (e.g., recruitment sources, message realism).

Events that occur as a choice is being made may well set the tone for future employee/employer relations. What little research exists on this topic is promising and suggests that this is a fertile area for exploration.

NOTES

1. The overall impact of recruitment is discussed at length in Chapter 5.
2. The concept of utility is discussed in more detail in Chapter 5.

5 Does Recruitment Matter?

THE ORGANIZATION'S PERSPECTIVE

In preceding chapters, I divided the recruitment process into separate stages and considered each independently. My objectives in choosing this structure were first, to clarify the process of recruitment by delineating its component phases and second, to find a logical means of organizing an increasingly voluminous literature.

But this approach has one significant disadvantage: It fails to provide an assessment of whether recruitment as a whole has a significant impact on organizational outcomes or, in other words, whether recruitment matters. What is the net impact of recruitment activities on organizations? Is recruitment sufficiently important to warrant additional research attention? The purpose of this chapter is to address questions of this sort by focusing on the recruitment process in its entirety.

In the preceding chapters, recruitment, although defined as an organizational activity, was examined primarily from the individual's point of view. Indeed, most recruitment literature deals with individual attitudes and behaviors associated with specific recruitment practices. Such an approach is warranted for at least two reasons. First, it is individual responses that, in aggregate, ultimately determine whether organizational recruitment is effective. Therefore, it is essential that we understand those individual level responses. Second, focus on the individual allows recruitment researchers to draw from psychological theory in framing research questions and in explaining observed relationships, adding a degree of richness to recruitment studies.

But one should not lose sight of the fact that recruitment is defined, here and elsewhere, as an organizational phenomenon. Recruitment is a set of activities conducted by an organization in hopes of identifying and attracting suitable employees, with the implicit distal goal of improving organizational performance. Thus, it is important to evaluate recruitment from an organizational perspective.

Several current trends reinforce the importance of addressing questions of this sort. First, human resource practitioners are increasingly being called upon to document the "value added" by their programs and policies, often in precise financial terms (e.g., Minnehan, 1997; Stewart, 1996). Second, human resource scholars have increasingly focused their attention on relationships between human resource policies and objective indicators of firm performance. For example, in 1996 a special issue of *The Academy of Management Journal* was devoted to the topic.

It is both appropriate, and timely, to consider recruitment's impact on the organization. It is also a difficult task, given the multiplicity of recruitment activities and the many possible intermediate processes through which these various activities might influence organizational outcomes. Typical recruitment research, in which a single aspect of recruitment (e.g., choice of source, realistic previews, campus interviews) is associated with one or perhaps two individual level outcomes (e.g., decision to accept an offer, duration of employment), can begin to suggest how recruitment might influence organizational performance. But the larger question of whether recruitment *as a whole* matters to organizations must be addressed in other ways.

Three approaches to answering the question "Does recruitment matter?" are examined in this chapter. First, the utility perspective on recruitment is reviewed. Second, research directly linking recruitment activities to firm performance measures is considered. Finally, studies that embrace a variety of recruitment activities and outcomes are discussed. It should be noted at the outset that there is little existing research in any of these categories, leaving a wealth of opportunity for future research.

Utility Models of Recruitment

One approach to assessing the impact recruitment can have on organizational outcomes involves *utility analysis*. As defined by Boudreau (1991), utility analysis refers to "the process that describes, predicts, and/or explains what determines the usefulness or desirability of decision options. . . " (p. 622), with decision options in this context referring to any of the various choices that are made in the design of a recruitment program. Landy, Farr, and Jacobs (1982) suggested that utility analysis models may be capable of generating "bottom line" evaluations of human resource practices.

Most existing utility analysis research has focused on selection models of utility (Boudreau, 1991). These models attempt to identify the "returns" (typically defined as productivity and expressed in dollar terms) associated with the use of different selection procedures. Many versions of these models exist. A relatively simple version is as follows:

(5.1) $$\Delta U = N r_{xy} S D_y Z_s - (NC)/p$$

where:

ΔU = the gain in utility (based on productivity improvements, and assessed in dollar terms) associated with using the selection device under consideration rather than hiring at random

N = the number of positions to be filled

r_{xy} = the validity coefficient associated with the selection device being considered

SD_y = the standard deviation of performance, expressed in dollar terms

Z_s = the average ability level of the applicants selected

C = the cost of selecting one applicant, and

p = the selection ratio (i.e., the proportion of applicants who receive offers).

The above equation suggests that, all else equal, the utility of a specific selection tool will be higher when there are many jobs to be filled; when the selection device is highly valid; when there is substantial variation in performance among different employees; and when the average ability level of those hired (i.e., their scores on the selection device) are high. Further, utility will be lower to the extent that selection costs are high and when only a small proportion of those screened are actually hired. This model, while fairly simple, is sufficient to understand the following arguments about how recruitment can have an effect on selection utility.

Within the realm of utility analysis research, the importance of recruitment has been introduced through selection utility models. Several authors have examined how recruitment issues might change utility estimates.

First, Hogarth and Einhorn (1976) and also Murphy (1986) noted that most selection utility estimates implicitly assume that all who are offered a job will accept it. This assumption is embedded in the Z_s term, which bases productivity on those *selected* rather than on those *actually hired* (i.e., those selectees who accept job offers). But as Murphy argued, in reality, job acceptance rates are well below 100%. Murphy noted that Z_s (average applicant ability) decreases to the extent that highly-rated applicants reject offers, causing the organization to reach down into the applicant pool and extend offers to lower-rated applicants. He examined three scenarios in estimating how the rejection of offers might influence utility estimates: First, when a number of individuals who are offered jobs reject them but rejections are unrelated to applicant quality; second, when jobs are rejected only by the best applicants; and third, when there is an imperfect relationship between applicant attractiveness and probability of rejecting the job. On the basis of these analyses, Murphy concluded that failure to consider the possibility that offers might be rejected can lead to overestimates of utility in the range of 30%-80%. From a recruitment standpoint, this suggests that selection utility can be substantially higher when the majority of applicants accept job offers, and that recruitment efforts aimed at ensuring that offers are accepted can have substantial payoffs.

Second, it has been argued that utility models considering selection costs but ignoring recruitment costs seriously underestimate the total costs of hiring and can lead to biased results. Martin and Raju (1992) cited data indicating that recruitment costs may actually exceed selection costs, and argued that it is therefore imperative that recruitment costs be included in utility models. They also argued that recruitment costs vary depending on the number of applicants needed. Employers needing only a few applicants may be able to rely exclusively on inexpensive recruitment sources, such as direct applications or employee referrals. If hiring needs are great, however, employers may need to go beyond these cost-effective sources and consider more expensive approaches, such as advertising or using placement agencies. Thus the cost of recruiting an additional applicant is not constant; rather, it increases as the number of applicants sought increases.

Martin and Raju (1992) incorporated an additional term into their utility model to reflect the variable costs of recruitment. Their modified equation is as follows:

$$(5.2) \qquad \Delta U = N r_{xy} S D_y Z_s - (NC)/p - N C_r)/p$$

where C_r represents the average cost of recruitment and increases continuously as the number of applicants required increases. They provide two examples of the impact this adjustment can have on the utility of selection, both of which demonstrate that recruitment costs can substantially alter estimates of utility and decisions about optimal hiring practices. In fact, in one example, what appeared to be an optimal choice based on a traditional selection utility model was demonstrated to have *negative* utility consequences after recruitment costs were considered.

Law and Myors (1993) supported the general argument that recruitment costs should be incorporated into assessments of utility but argued that recruitment costs should be presented as a step function rather than as a continuous function. For example, suppose that an organization can attract 10 applicants via direct application and that a newspaper advertisement yields an additional 50 applicants. In this scenario, the recruitment costs associated with attracting 11 applicants rather than 10 would be identical to the recruitment costs associated with attracting 12, or 20, or 60 applicants rather than 10. In other words, the cost per hire would not increase continuously. Law and Myors (1993) also recommended a focus on interval estimates, rather than point estimates, of the number of applicants required to maximize selection utilities. These modifications illustrate the complexity of attempting to account for recruitment costs in utility models but at the same time illustrate the importance of doing so. And, as Law and Myors (1993) noted, their treatment of recruitment costs is actually a simplification, as it includes only source use costs and ignores other costs associated with processing applicants.

Boudreau and Rynes (1985) provided the most thorough treatment of recruitment utility issues that currently exists. They argued that recruitment can influence many of the parameters of traditional utility models, and suggested that recruitment's impact on utility is not merely a function of recruitment costs. They noted that one of the primary objectives of recruitment is to modify the characteristics of the applicants who will be screened. In other words, recruiters are not merely interested in increasing the number of applicants but are also interested in increasing applicant quality. As a result, recruitment can influence selection device validity (r_{xy}), performance variation (SD_y), and average ability level of hirees (Z_s). They provide numerical illustrations of these effects, demonstrating that utility estimates can vary dramatically depending on, first, whether recruitment issues are even considered, and second, what types of recruitment practices are used. Boudreau and Rynes (1985) called for research examining how specific recruitment practices (e.g., sources used, nature of recruitment message, administrative procedures) might be related to these parameters as a means of improving the accuracy of utility estimates. Their suggestions are particularly helpful in that they emphasize the need to consider multiple aspects of recruitment in evaluating its total effects. Yet little attention has been paid to these issues in the decade since their paper was published.

Indeed, to a degree the utility analysis approach to assessing human resource management has been supplanted by other perspectives. As Becker and Gerhart (1996) noted, utility analysis estimates tend to have broad confidence intervals and are not highly robust to changes in assumptions. Furthermore, Boudreau (1991) acknowledged that even the most complex utility models fail to incorporate all relevant attributes and, as a result, do not really capture the impact of human resource programs; instead, Boudreau argued, they are best viewed as decision-making tools. Latham and Whyte (1994), however, demonstrated that managers did not use utility estimates to support their decisions regarding selection procedures. Instead, utility's impact was negative: Managers were less likely to implement valid selection procedures when utility information was provided. Latham and Whyte suggested that this negative impact may have been due to a lack of credibility associated with very large estimates of dollar gains. Overall, then, it is not surprising that more recent attempts to assess the actual impact of human resource management practices (including recruitment) have not employed utility models.

Recruitment and Organizational Effectiveness

In recent years, there has been a significant change in human resource management practice and research. The emergence of strategic human resource management (SHRM) as a professional orientation and as a topic of research has shifted at least some scholarly attention away from traditional individual-level analyses to more macro or organization-level analyses. A critical assumption underlying this work is that human resource practices can influence objective indicators of firm performance, such as profitability, stock prices, and even survival. These effects are expected to occur through intervening variables more directly related to human resource issues, such as productivity and turnover (Becker & Gerhart, 1996; Huselid, 1995). A growing body of empirical literature demonstrates the existence of relationships between human resource practices and organization-level outcomes (e.g., Arthur, 1994; Huselid, 1995; MacDuffie, 1995; Wellbourne & Andrews, 1996). One advantage of this approach is that by focusing on final outcomes, it captures effects that occur through any number of possible intermediate outcomes. For example, from a recruitment perspective, recruitment influences on any actor (applicants, organization members, or outsiders) will be reflected in the assessment of firm performance. Unfortunately, relatively few firm performance studies have focused in any detail on recruitment.

Schmitt and Schneider (1983) were among the earliest to suggest that research associating personnel selection with organizational effectiveness was necessary. They argued that such work was necessary to assess selection's effectiveness relative to other management interventions, and also to compare the relative effectiveness of organizations using different selection procedures. They provided an agenda for such research that included three principle steps: identifying criteria of importance to organizations that might be related to selection practices (e.g., turnover rates, productivity, market share, sales growth); randomly selecting a large group of organizations and assessing their human resource practices as well as their performance on the chosen criteria; and measuring association between human resource practices and criteria. Obviously, this model can be extended beyond selection practices and applied to staffing practices more generally defined or to recruitment in particular.

One study that directly responded to Schmitt and Schneider's (1983) recommendations was conducted by Terpstra and Rozell. Terpstra and Rozell (1993) surveyed 201 companies regarding five staffing practices (evaluation of recruiting sources, validation studies, structured interviews, cognitive tests, and biographical information blanks) and examined associations between use of those practices and firm performance. Of particular interest here is the relationship between whether recruiting sources were evaluated and firm performance. Terpstra and Rozell found some association between these variables, although effects varied by industry. Source evaluation was associated with higher annual profit in the manufacturing sector, with sales growth and overall firm performance in the service sector, and with annual profit and overall performance among wholesale/retail firms. Source evaluation was unrelated to organizational performance measures within the financial industry.

Delaney and Huselid (1996) provide additional evidence regarding recruitment's effect on the bottom line. Using a sample of 590 firms from the National Organizations Survey, they assessed whether the ratio of applicants to job openings (a measure of recruitment intensity) was associated with informants' perceptions of organizational performance. They found that recruitment intensity was unrelated to perceived organizational performance, a broad measure incorporating issues such as product quality, customer satisfaction, and new product development. Recruitment intensity, however, was significantly and positively related to perceived market performance, a measure focusing on economic outcomes, such as profitability and market share.

Though many other studies of the relationship between human resource practices and firm performance have been conducted (generally with positive results), they generally shed little light on recruitment issues per se. First, although recruitment has been identified as a key practice by a number of scholars (e.g., Huselid, 1995; MacDuffie, 1995; Pfeffer, 1994), it is not always included in studies of human resource policies' impact on firm performance. Second, because many of the studies are concerned with examining the impact of integrated programs or bundles of human resource policies (e.g., Arthur, 1994; Huselid, 1995; MacDuffie, 1995), it is often impossible to disentangle the results of individual policies, such as those related to recruitment.

Thus we are left with severely limited, but promising, data on the impact of recruitment on the "bottom line."

Expanding the Traditional
Recruitment Research Approach

One acknowledged shortcoming of research associating HR policies with financial performance outcomes is that it sheds little light on exactly how these effects are obtained. Becker and Gerhart (1996) noted that "(f)uture work on the strategic perspective must elaborate on the black box between a firm's HR system and the firm's bottom line" (p. 793). Huselid (1995) provided some movement in this direction by demonstrating that HR policies influence firm performance at least in part through their effect on turnover and productivity. Yet even this tells us little about the mechanisms by which such policies result in bottom-line consequences.

Fortunately, traditional individual-level research can help fill this gap. Material reviewed in the preceding chapters suggests how specific recruitment practices can lead to individual or organizational performance outcomes, and can be used to build and test comprehensive models of recruitment effects. By designing studies that assess the effects of a greater number of activities on a greater variety of outcomes, we can improve our understanding of recruitment's total impact without moving terribly far from our traditional research paradigm.

In this section, I propose research designs that address two different questions about the impact of recruitment. The first focuses on recruitment's' effect on the individual. This approach conceptualizes recruitment as a set of policies designed to influence a series of individual applicant decisions and behaviors. To understand recruitment's total effect in this sense, we must study relationships between the full complement of recruitment activities and the full spectrum of choices and behaviors through which individuals either do or do not become productive members of an organization. This suggested approach retains the individual focus typical of much recruitment research but expands investigations to include a variety of recruitment activities and outcomes across multiple stages.

The second approach represents a somewhat greater departure from current research in that it conceptualizes recruitment as a set of policies designed to influence *organizational* recruitment outcomes and therefore uses the organization as the unit of analysis. To understand recruitment's effects in this sense, we must study relationships between a variety of recruitment activities and outcome measures at the organizational level. In the following sections, these approaches are discussed in more detail.

Longitudinal Individual-Level Research

One way to think about recruitment is as a process in which applicants move through various stages, making decisions (e.g., whether to apply, whether to persist, whether to accept an offer) at various points along the way. The purpose of recruitment is to influence those individual decisions in ways that are ultimately advantageous to the company. From this perspective, understanding the total effect of recruitment is a matter of assessing the cumulative influence of varied recruitment activities as applicants flow through the recruitment process.

This approach requires longitudinal research designs, including wide ranges of recruitment activities and outcomes. Ideally, data would be collected from applicants (or potential applicants) at all critical decision points, and might include both affective reactions and actual decisions or behaviors. In addition, at each of these points, data would be collected regarding the applicants' most recent recruitment experiences. For example, during the first phase of recruitment, decisions regarding whether to apply for a given job would be measured, as would the organization's image, various aspects of recruitment materials, and the source through which the potential applicant was contacted. During the second phase, decisions regarding whether to continue pursuing the job would be measured, along with information about initial interviews, later recruitment events, and selection procedures. Later, job choices could be measured, along with information about offer negotiations, job attributes, and alternative opportunities.

This approach has several advantages for exploring the effects of recruitment. First, it would allow us to look at recruitment as a process, evaluating applicant withdrawal that occurs early, as well as late, in the process. As argued earlier, the loss of qualified applicants early in the recruitment process is no less serious than the loss of such applicants later on. Though it may not be possible to aggregate effects from various phases into a single numerical assessment of recruitment's effect, findings that recruitment matters at multiple phases would go far to document recruitment's importance.

In addition, such a design could provide information about the degree to which recruitment effects carry over from one stage to another, in other words, whether a specific recruitment activity might have both proximal and distal consequences. For instance, does company image retain its importance as applicants learn more about the organization? Do reactions to campus recruiters influence applicants after they have met with other organizational representatives (e.g., a site visit host)? Ideally, we would also be able to assess the mechanisms by which distal effects (if any) occur—in particular, whether they are mediated by earlier outcomes.

Not surprisingly, few recruitment scholars have undertaken the massive data collection efforts required by this research approach. Taylor and Bergmann (1987), however, used a design very similar to that proposed. Their study is used to demonstrate both the advantages and the frustrations associated with such research.

Taylor & Bergmann (1987)

Taylor and Bergmann (1987) studied the effect of a single organization's recruitment activities on applicants at five points: immediately following campus interviews; during the period between campus interviews and site visits; following site visits; at the time an offer was extended; and at the time job choice decisions were made. A wide variety of recruitment variables were assessed, including variables relating to the campus interview, the site visit, and various general administrative procedures. Table 5.1 summarizes their data collection procedures.

Taylor and Bergmann had two primary hypotheses: first, that job applicant reactions would be influenced by job attributes, and second, that they would be influenced by recruitment activities. In addition, they hypothesized that the strength of recruitment effects would vary as a function of offer characteristics (how similar this offer was to others), applicant characteristics (how much work experience they had), and labor market opportunities (how many alternative opportunities applicants had). They concluded that recruitment's effects were largely limited to the earliest stages of the process, and that at later points perceptions of job attributes explained far more variance in applicant reactions than did recruiting practices. They also found little evidence that the strength of recruitment effects varied as predicted.

This study made several important contributions to the literature. First, it was one of the earliest studies to consider recruitment activi-

Table 5.1   MEASURES AND DATA COLLECTION: TAYLOR & BERGMANN 1987

ONSTRUCT MEASURED	Number of items	Time 1	Time 2	Time 3	Time 4	Time 5
DEPENDENT VARIABLES:						
Company attractiveness	4	x	x	x	x	x
Probability of offer acceptance	2	x		x	x	
Job offer decision	1					x
Tenure intentions	6					x
INDEPENDENT VARIABLES:						
1. Initial interview:						
Recruiter characteristics	8	x				
Nature of interview:						
(as assessed by recruiter)	16	x				
(as assessed by applicant)	13	x				
2. Nature of communication following initial interview	4		x			
3. Site Visit:						
Advance Arrangements	9			x		
Visit itself	10			x		
4. Offer extension process	15				x	x
5. Job attributes	31				x	x
6. Moderating (context) variables	11	x	x	x	x	x
7. Sample size		910	507	95	91	38

ties that occurred after the initial campus interview, and remains one of the only studies to investigate the effect of the process by which job offers are extended. Second, it provided a rich context for studying recruitment effects by incorporating job attributes as alternative influences on applicants and by studying factors expected to moderate reactions to recruitment. Third, it represents an ambitious attempt to collect longitudinal data and investigate effects over time, though sample shrinkage severely impaired the authors' abilities to carry out true longitudinal analyses, as discussed in more detail below.

Difficulties Encountered in Longitudinal Research[1]

Very few recruitment studies have adopted research designs as ambitious as that of Taylor and Bergmann. This is no doubt due in part to the difficulties associated with conducting such research. Some of the most likely difficulties are described below.

Sample size and subject attrition. Table 5.1 provides sample sizes for each stage of Taylor and Bergmann's research. As is common in longitudinal research, substantial shrinkage occurred over the course of the study: The initial campus interview survey was completed by 910 subjects, but the job offer decision survey was completed by only 38. This shrinkage occurred despite the authors' efforts to boost their sample at later stages by including new subjects.

Subject attrition, and the resulting reduction in sample size, affects our ability to analyze and interpret results in several ways. First, because very few subjects participated in all five surveys, Taylor and Bergmann were unable to test truly longitudinal models. Instead, they used a series of regression analyses to estimate the influence of recruitment activities on applicant reactions *within stages,* in effect providing five different cross-sectional views of recruitment's effect rather than a longitudinal view.

This approach represents an improvement over studies that focus on a specific stage (or activity) in that comparisons across stages can be made. For example, Taylor and Bergmann compared the influence of early recruitment activities on early reactions to the influence of later recruitment activities on later reactions, and concluded that recruitment's effects occur primarily early on. Sample shrinkage, however, can make such comparisons difficult if not misleading, particularly if one relies on statistical significance as the sole indicator of an effect's importance. The substantial variation in sample size across time periods (from 910 to 38) results in greater power to find significant results at early stages than at later stages. Examination of effect sizes indicates that some of the later recruitment activities explain greater amounts of variation in dependent variables than do the earlier activities. For instance, almost 10% of the variance in intention to remain with the employer was explained by how one was treated during the decision period (a nonsignificant effect), while statistically significant early effects accounted for only 1 or 2% of the variance in early attraction to the organization. It is not entirely clear that small significant effects found in large samples are in any practical sense more "important" than larger nonsignificant effects found in small samples. Comparisons across stages, then, must be made with a great deal of caution.

Maintaining adequate sample sizes throughout the duration of a longitudinal project would obviously improve our ability to interpret results across stages. It would also allow us to systematically examine whether effects carry over across stages. However, this objective is far more easily stated than accomplished. Taylor and Bergmann, as described above, "boosted" their sample at later stages by including new subjects, and also engaged in extensive monitoring and follow-up activities. Unfortunately, a dramatic change in the host organization's hiring plans during this project curtailed the number of participants being recruited, reducing the number of subjects available to be surveyed. Thus, even good planning and hard work were insufficient to maintain sample size. Taylor (personal communication, July 1997) recommended that in the future, researchers undertaking this kind of research should consider identifying host organizations in growing industries (to reduce the possibility of curtailed recruitment) and be more aggressive in attempting to persuade rejected candidates to respond to surveys, perhaps through providing some sort of inducement.

In addition, researchers interested in conducting longitudinal studies should investigate sophisticated statistical approaches, such as survival analysis, that are well suited to handling longitudinal data. Survival analysis comprises a set of techniques designed to analyze events that occur over time (such as the decision to choose, or reject, a job). One advantage of survival analysis is that it can incorporate "censored" data, in other words, data from individuals who did not reach the final point of the study (in this case, job choice) for involuntary reasons (e.g., because the company did not extend an offer). This may ameliorate problems associated with subject attrition. Researchers interested in survival analysis and its application to management topics are encouraged to read Morita, Lee, and Mowday (1989).

Other data collection issues. Maintaining subject participation is certainly a problem for those conducting longitudinal research, but it is not the only difficulty encountered. A second problem is determining when to gather data. For example, job choice can only be assessed after a choice has been made. But post-choice dissonance reduction may distort data collected too long after choice. Thus the decision of exactly when to send out surveys is more difficult than it might appear. Perhaps the best thing researchers can do here is to work closely with individuals or organizations familiar with the timing of the labor market being studied to set reasonable and realistic dates for the distribution of surveys. Employment intermediaries (such as placement offices or search firms) may be good sources of information regarding when the various recruitment stages begin and end for their clients. Alternatively, focusing on a single organization (as Taylor and Bergmann did) would allow surveys to be coordinated with recruitment practices, as a single organization will know exactly when campus interviews or site visits were conducted and when offers were extended.

An additional challenge stems from the fact that research covering multiple stages of recruitment requires measurement of a wide variety of recruitment activities and outcomes. Table 5.1, which lists variables measured by Taylor and Bergmann, illustrates this point. Therefore researchers need to design surveys that are clear, simple, not overly long, yet still capture essential information. Several recommendations can be offered with respect to this issue. First, identification or development of short yet reliable instruments for measuring individual variables is essential. Second, variables should be selected carefully. Rather than include all possible activities and outcomes, researchers should examine existing within-stage research to identify the most promising candidates for inclusion.

Single organization or multiple organizations? Taylor and Bergmann worked with a single host organization in designing their study. This approach has several advantages. One advantage, mentioned earlier, is that survey timing can be based on the organization's recruitment schedule. A second advantage is that organizational sponsorship of the project may lead to greater subject participation. A third advantage is that many nonrecruitment factors that could influence attraction to the organization are "controlled" by using a single organization.

However, the single-organization approach also has drawbacks. First, there is the question of whether results can be generalized to other organizations. All organizations have idiosyncrasies, and choosing a "representative" organization is essentially impossible. Though this problem is difficult to get around, descriptions of the company in which the study was based can help readers judge whether results are likely to generalize to other specific contexts or not. Researchers should also heed Johns's (1993) recommendation that actual company names be used whenever feasible to provide readers with a better sense of the research context.

A second possible drawback associated with the single-organization approach is that there may be little variation in recruitment practices within an organization, and that lack of variation may lead to an underestimation of recruitment's effect. Taylor and Bergmann found substantial variation within their organization, presumably because recruitment activities were largely decentralized. Nevertheless, it remains likely that recruitment practices differ more across organizations than within.

In summary, longitudinal individual-level recruitment research poses a number of data collection and analysis challenges but they are not insurmountable. Such research has the potential to add greatly to our understanding of recruitment as a process, and would provide a more complete picture of how individuals respond to recruitment. It does not, however, address the question of how recruitment influences organizational outcomes. Research directed toward that question is proposed below.

Cross-Sectional Organization-Level Research

To date, relatively little recruitment research has taken the organization's perspective or, more specifically, used the organization as the unit of analysis. Rynes and Barber (1990) offered a series of propositions dealing with attraction issues at the organizational level, but few of these have actually been tested. Instead, research has focused on the individual. The few studies that focus on organizational issues in recruitment tend to be primarily descriptive (e.g., Rynes & Boudreau, 1986; Rynes, Orlitsky & Bretz, 1997).

Yet cross-sectional multi-organization studies can provide a wealth of information about the effect of recruitment activities. Such research could examine whether variations in recruitment practices are associated with differences in immediate recruitment outcomes, such as applicant pool size and composition, acceptance rates, and time required to fill positions, which could in turn be associated with more distal outcomes, such as productivity or turnover. In the following section, a study by Williams and Dreher (1992) that did assess organizational recruitment outcomes is used to demonstrate the advantages and disadvantages of such research.

Williams & Dreher (1992)

Williams and Dreher (1992) studied the relationship between compensation policies and recruitment outcomes in a sample of 352 U.S. banks. Compensation policies, of course, are job attributes and not recruitment practices per se. Compensation can be, and is, manipulated for recruitment purposes, however (Rynes, 1986; Tully, 1996), and such manipulations are within the domain of recruitment as defined in this book.

Williams and Dreher assessed relationships between compensation policies as applied to bank tellers and three recruitment outcomes: applicant pool size (i.e., number of applicants), acceptance rates (i.e., the percentage of offers that were accepted), and the number of days required to fill positions. They concluded that applicant pool size was positively associated with the percentage of compensation allocated for benefits, that acceptance rates were positively associated with pay level, and that days required to fill positions was negatively associated with benefits level. They also found, contrary to expectations, that applicant pool size was negatively related to benefit flexibility (firms that offered flexible benefits had), and that days required to fill a position was positively related to pay level (firms that paid more took longer to fill positions).

This approach to investigating compensation's effect on recruitment outcomes could easily be applied to the study of recruitment practices in general. One should not be misled by the apparent simplicity of this design, however. In fact, cross-sectional organization research presents a number of methodological difficulties, as discussed below.

Difficulties Encountered in Cross-Sectional Research[2]

Response rates. One difficulty frequently encountered in large-scale surveys of organizations is low response rates. A large number of nonrespondents is problematic for several reasons. First, they reduce the size of the sample available for analysis. Second, they raise concerns about bias in that the decision not to respond may be systematically related to the issues being studied. In their study, Williams and Dreher obtained a response rate of 33%. This rate is actually fairly high for organizational survey research; response rates of 20% or less are not uncommon in the published literature. Several approaches to improving response rates that should be considered by cross-sectional researchers include extensive follow-up (e.g., through second mailings), provision of incentives to respondents, and streamlined survey construction (based on the assumption that surveys that are short or otherwise easy to complete are more likely to be returned than long or difficult surveys).

Confounding factors. A second difficulty concerns the likelihood that unmeasured variables might hinder interpretation of findings. Recruitment outcomes are likely influenced by a variety of forces, some of which are intended to affect outcomes and others whose significance is unanticipated or at least unplanned. A challenge in conducting cross-sectional research is to ensure that study results are not biased by important but unmeasured variables. Various means can be used to protect this form of bias. First, one can limit the study to organizations of a certain type to eliminate variation on organizational characteristics. For example, by including only banks in their sample, Williams and Dreher eliminated the possibility that results could be attributed to industry or sector. Second, one can measure variables that, although not directly involved in the study's hypotheses, might be expected to influence recruitment outcomes. Variance attributable to these factors can then be statistically controlled. Williams and Dreher used statistical control to account for the influence of labor market characteristics, such as unemployment rates and average pay levels, as well as firm characteristics, such as size.

An alternative approach to controlling for influences external to the firm is to conduct pre- and post-test studies of the effect of specific recruitment procedures on organizational level recruitment outcomes within a single firm. Such designs are difficult in that they require researchers to find organizations that have adequate outcome data both before and after the change, or to actually be involved with the organization prior to change. In addition, establishing adequate internal validity, through identification of a control group, for example, is always difficult in field studies. But this approach is not infeasible. It has, for instance, been used successfully in compensation research (e.g., Barber, Dunham, & Formisano, 1992; Brown & Huber, 1992).

Assessing causality. A third difficulty associated with cross-sectional research involves causality. When data are collected at a single point in time, it is impossible to assess the direction of causality between two variables. In the case of recruitment practices and outcomes, it is certainly plausible that firms adopting effective practices would experience good outcomes—in other words, that practices cause outcomes. On the other hand, it is also quite plausible that firms experiencing negative recruitment outcomes would change their recruitment practices to become more effective—in other words, that outcomes cause practices. Williams and Dreher noted that this reactance may have provided the explanation for some of their counterintuitive findings—for example, that firms offering higher pay levels were not able to fill jobs as quickly as firms offering lower pay levels.

There is little that can be done to resolve this issue within the confines of a single survey. Williams and Dreher, however, collected additional data to verify their explanation. They collected follow-up data on compensation policies, and tested whether recruitment outcomes on the initial survey could predict compensation policies on the later survey. Their evidence supported the reactance explanation: Organizations that took longer to fill jobs at the time of the first survey offered higher pay at the time of the second survey.

Measurement issues. A final concern in cross-sectional organizational surveys involves measurement. Typically, these surveys are sent to a single respondent, and the accuracy of that person's responses is hard to verify. They may not have access to requested information, or their beliefs about recruitment practices and outcomes may be biased by their own stake in recruitment. Several approaches are available to assess the quality of responses, though none is ideal. First, when available, archival data can be used to verify the accuracy of responses. Second, documentation of recruitment or other human resource policies (e.g., relevant portions of policy manuals or other corporate communications) can be requested. Third, and perhaps most important, multiple respondents can be used (Kumar, Stern, and Anderson, 1993).

Conclusion

This chapter described several alternative approaches to studying recruitment issues from the organization's perspective. To date, little recruitment research has employed any of these approaches, and there is much room to contribute to the knowledge base. Each approach to assessing recruitment's total effect has its own advantages and disadvantages. As a result, it is unreasonable to argue that any one of the approaches described above is vastly superior to others, and more appropriate to suggest that studies using any of these approaches are needed.

The need for more organization-oriented research does not imply that there is no need for additional individual-oriented research. The ability to draw from a rich literature on applicant reactions to specific recruitment practices is a real advantage for researchers interested in recruitment's overall effect, as that literature can be used to formulate logical, parsimonious models on the basis of empirical evidence and conceptual argument. But, as previous chapters demonstrate, many unanswered questions remain about the effect of specific recruitment activities on individuals. Research addressing those questions can enrich the study of organizational outcomes.

Indeed, to a great extent, "macro" (organizational) and "micro" (individual) research streams should complement one another. Organizational-level research can help us identify practices and procedures that lead to outcomes of practical importance; individual-level research can help us understand why or how organization-level results are obtained. Both make important contributions to recruitment research.

NOTES

1. This section is based in part on recent conversations with Susan Taylor. Her generosity in recalling difficulties associated with this project is appreciated.
2. My thanks to Peg Williams for her insights on this issue.

6 Toward an Agenda for Recruitment Research

```
Key dimensions of recruitment: What do we know?
      Actors
      Activities
      Outcomes
      Context
      Phases
  Guidelines for Future Research
  Concluding Remarks
```

In previous chapters, specific recruitment research topics were examined in detail, and recommendations for future research on those topics were made. The purpose of this chapter is to take a broader view of recruitment research, offering recommendations about general areas of, or approaches to, recruitment research that might best move the field forward. In the first part of the chapter, I return to the key dimensions of recruitment identified in Chapter 1, and discuss how well existing research has addressed or incorporated these elements. In the second part, I propose guidelines for future research.

Key Dimensions of Recruitment: What Do We Know?

Actors

Table 6.1 lists the four key actors identified in Chapter 1, and provides a summary evaluation of our knowledge of their roles in recruitment.

Table 6.1:   What we know about actors

ACTOR	EVALUATION OF CURRENT KNOWLEDGE BASE
Applicants	Substantial information available; generally the focal point of research
Organizations	Little understanding of their actions; better understanding of how they are affected
Organizational agents	Often treated as passive; rarely considered as unique actors
Outsiders	Minimal knowledge of potential effects

The vast majority of recruitment research has focused on applicants and their reactions to the process. At this time, we know something about how they react to recruitment materials, interviews, and other recruitment procedures; we also have fairly good information about how (and why) they choose jobs. This past emphasis on applicants is not inappropriate, as the primary objective of recruitment is, after all, to influence applicants.

This focus, however, results in a rather incomplete understanding of the recruitment process. Though we have some understanding of how organizations are affected by recruitment (for instance, how realistic job previews influence turnover rates), we know almost nothing about organizations *as actors* in recruitment. Rynes and Barber (1990) offered a lengthy list of propositions regarding how organizations might make decisions about recruitment and attraction practices, but to date little research has been conducted along those lines.

We have even less research focusing on the actions of organizational agents—those individuals who carry out the organization's recruitment strategies.With the exception of some work by Stevens (1990, in press), most research either treats agents as passive actors or fails to differentiate them from the organization itself. For example, though many have studied applicant reactions to recruiter behaviors, few have studied whether or how recruiters might be persuaded to modify their behaviors to enhance recruitment effectiveness. The lack of research taking the agents' perspective is a potentially serious omission, as one cannot presume that agents—whether recruiters, site visit hosts, those involved in making and negotiating offers, or others—are willing or able to behave in a manner consistent with the organization's goals and intentions. Additional research along these lines could have substantial practical value.

Finally, few studies have addressed the potential for recruitment activities to "spill over" and influence parties not directly involved in the recruitment process. Though the public relations aspect of recruitment is frequently acknowledged, it is rarely assessed. It seems likely that spillover effects are most common during early stages of recruitment, when recruitment messages are broadly disseminated. Therefore, it is unfortunate that we do not know whether or how nonapplicants respond to recruitment advertisements or attempts to manipulate organizational image—for instance, whether their decisions to purchase goods from the organization or to invest in the organization are affected. Nor do we know to what extent the "campus grapevine" circulates information about ineffective recruiters and discourages potential applicants. What little information we do have about spillover effects comes from later stages of recruitment: there is evidence that applicant reactions to selection procedures are associated with their willingness to recommend the employer to others (Smither et al., 1993) and weakly associated with intentions to buy the employer's product (Macan et al., 1994). An improved understanding of recruitment's spillover effects would lead to improved understanding of recruitment's total influence on organizations.

Activities

Table 6.2 provides an overview of what we know about various recruitment activities.

With respect to recruitment activities, the bulk of the existing literature focuses on two elements: choice of medium/source and message delivery. With respect to recruitment sources, the longer-term consequences of source choice such as relationships between recruitment sources and turnover have been studied extensively, but we know fairly little about relationships between recruitment sources and more proximal outcomes such as applicant attraction. With respect to message delivery, we know a great deal about how applicants respond to specific messengers (e.g., campus recruiters) and to various types of messages (e.g., reactions to RJPs, reactions to recruitment materials).Our attention, however, has primarily been directed toward initial recruitment contacts such as campus interviews; other means of delivering the recruitment message (such as site visits) have been investigated less often.

In contrast, we have very little research on recruitment activities that occur either very early (e.g., defining target applicants) or very late (e.g., extending offers) in the process. Certainly, these activities are important. Early activities influence the quality and quantity of applicants who can be recruited later. Later activities are particularly important in that they focus on those individuals the organization

Table 6.2   What we know about activities

ACTIVITY	EVALUATION OF CURRENT KNOWLEDGE BASE
Defining a target population	Almost no information
Choice of source/medium	Some knowledge of consequences of choice
Message delivery	Substantial information on some topics
Closing the deal	Some knowledge of why and how applicants choose jobs but little understanding of recruitment activities dealing specifically with job offers/choice
Administrative processes	Limited knowledge on some issues

Table 6.3:   What we know about outcomes

OUTCOMES	EVALUATION OF CURRENT KNOWLEDGE BASE
Attraction	Good understanding of effects of some aspects of recruitment, e.g. reactions to recruiters; little understanding of effects of other aspects, e.g. image
Post-Hire outcomes	Good understanding of effects of some aspects of recruitment, e.g. RJPs and sources; little understanding of effects of other aspects, e.g. recruitment activities subsequent to initial interviews
Organizational performance	Little knowledge
Other outcomes	Relatively little knowledge of long-term impact on agents or other employees

most wants to hire. Therefore, it is unclear why these activities have received relatively little research attention.

Outcomes

An overview of our current understanding of recruitment outcomes is provided in Table 6.3.

With respect to attraction and post-hire outcomes, the recruitment literature can best be described as unbalanced. Specific activities are studied in conjunction with specific outcomes. For example, interviews are typically studied from an attraction standpoint, but recruitment sources and communication realism are typically investigated in terms of post-hire behaviors such as turnover. Overall, outcomes involving individual behaviors (whether pre- or post-hire) have received substantially more attention than aggregated, organization-level outcomes. Neither organization-level recruitment outcomes (e.g., cost-per-hire, time required to fill positions) or more general organizational outcomes (e.g., firm performance) have been the focus of much recruitment research. In addition, research has largely ignored outcomes experienced by organizational agents or other employees.

Again, the focus on outcomes closely associated with individual applicants is neither surprising nor necessarily troubling, as recruitment is intended to influence applicants. There is room for debate, however, regarding whether recruitment research should address immediate outcomes such as application decisions, or pursue more distal outcomes such as post-hire behavior. This issue is addressed in more detail in Guideline #1 (below). Furthermore, as both practitioners and academics are increasingly being called upon to justify the practical importance of their work, one cannot ignore the importance of understanding recruitment's influence on organizational outcomes.

Context

According to Rynes (1991), important aspects of the recruitment context include internal factors (such as organizational characteristics and norms) and external factors (such as labor markets and legal regulations). To what extent does current recruitment research take internal or external context issues into consideration? Table 6.4 provides a rather bleak response to this question.

By and large, the recruitment literature has not been particularly successful in attending to context issues. Little attention has been paid to internal organizational factors, such as the organization's business strategy or the overall attractiveness of its jobs. Nor do we know much about how recruitment issues vary across industries or across occupations. But these factors could be important determinants of organizational choices regarding recruitment practices. They also could be important moderators of the effectiveness of specific recruitment practices. This inattention to organizational context may simply reflect how infrequently recruitment research is approached from the organization's perspective, and therefore may not be remedied until researchers pay more attention to the organization as an actor in recruitment.

Factors external to the organization have also received scant attention in the recruitment literature. Most disturbing is the fact that the influence of labor market forces on recruitment strategies and recruitment effectiveness has largely been ignored. It seems quite likely that

Table 6.4:   What we know about context

CONTEXT ISSUES	EVALUATION OF CURRENT KNOWLEDGE BASE
Internal	Almost no knowledge
External	Almost no knowledge

recruitment goals and outcomes will differ across tight versus loose labor markets. In addition, recruitment practices and outcomes may differ significantly depending on the structure and norms of different labor markets. For example, campus placement markets, which typically bring together soon-to-be college graduates and relatively large employers, tend to be characterized by long lead times (offers extended well before anticipated start dates) and the potential to accumulate and choose from multiple offers. Markets involving small employers or experienced hires may be less likely to permit the accumulation of offers, a factor that might well alter the role of recruitment. This suggests that the dangers of relying too heavily on campus placement settings as research sites are twofold: it focuses our attention not only on a particular kind of applicant but also on a particular kind of labor market.

Overall, then, we know little about how the context in which recruitment occurs influences its impact. This shortcoming is unfortunate, as it limits our ability to either understand or predict outcomes in the context-rich "real world." The problem can be addressed in several ways. First, recruitment researchers can (and should) provide detailed information about the context in which their research was conducted, describing the nature of the organization(s) involved as well as the type of labor market studied. This information would enrich our understanding of individual studies, and at the same time would facilitate meta-analyses examining the role of contextual factors *across* studies. Second, individual studies could systematically examine context issues, for example by simultaneously studying different labor markets.

Phases

Table 6.5 summarizes our current knowledge of the three phases of recruitment.

Table 6.5:   What we know about phases

PHASES	EVALUATION OF CURRENT KNOWLEDGE BASE
Generating Applicants	Significant knowledge of some issues, e.g. recruitment source effects; little or no knowledge of others, e.g. image
Maintaining Applicant Status	Focus of most recruitment research, but little attention to anything beyond the initial interview
Influencing job choice	Significant knowledge of some issues, e.g. choice process; little or no knowledge of others, e.g. impact of post-offer recruitment activities

The largest volume of recruitment research has focused on the middle stage, after potential applicants have formally applied to the company but before job offers are extended. Within this stage, the initial interview has received the most attention, and there is room for additional research on activities occurring later in this stage. The early stage of recruitment has received substantially less attention, and many important questions remain regarding this phase. For instance, as noted above, we know very little about applicant targeting or about the role of organizational image in attracting applicants. Similarly, significant research questions remain regarding the later stage of recruitment, when offers have been extended and acceptances must be obtained. In particular, virtually no research has focused on the effect of organizational recruitment activities that occur during this phase. Recruitment does not end when an offer is extended—in fact, it may become especially important at this stage—and recruitment research should reflect this continuing role.

Guidelines for Future Research

The summaries provided above and the preceding chapters identify a number of gaps in the recruitment literature. There is no shortage of unanswered questions pertaining to recruitment. The challenge is to identify and address research questions that will contribute in important ways to the accumulated body of recruitment knowledge. Toward this end, in the remainder of this chapter I propose a set of guidelines to be used in prioritizing future research.

Guideline #1: Focus on attraction

As noted above, recruitment can have many effects: on individuals and on organizations, and both pre-hire and post-hire. Interestingly, much existing recruitment research focuses on post-hire (distal) outcomes, such as performance and turnover, paying only passing attention to the more immediate and direct outcome of attraction. This occurs despite the fact that many factors, both individual and organizational, intervene between recruitment and post-hire outcomes. Recruitment scholars are beginning to question the wisdom of this focus. As Rynes (1991) argued, we "need to accord the immediate objective of recruitment—applicant attraction—higher priority" (p. 435). This redirection of effort offers several advantages. From a theoretical perspective, it is probable that recruitment will have stronger effects on proximal (pre-hire) than on distal (post-hire) outcomes. Further, to the extent that post-hire outcomes are affected by recruitment, such effects may well occur through the more immediate attraction outcomes. Thus examination of proximal effects seems more likely to generate useful knowledge about both short- and long-term consequences of recruitment.

From an applied perspective, it is not clear to what extent recruitment practices are actually *intended* to influence post-hire outcomes. Indeed, organizations have many other means of influencing post-hire outcomes, and may prefer to focus their recruitment efforts on initial attraction. As discussed earlier, we know little about organizational strategies or intentions with respect to recruitment. Such knowledge would help us assess the practical value of studying immediate versus longer-term outcomes. In the absence of such information, however, it is unwise to ignore either type of outcome. Given the tendency to focus on longer-term outcomes in the existing literature, redirection of research in the direction of attraction might be needed to develop a more balanced knowledge base.

Guideline #2: Focus on individual phases

The various phases of recruitment described above present complications for recruitment researchers. There are at least three ways to recognize the multistage nature of recruitment in our research. The first two, discussed in Chapter 5, involve either longitudinal research that cuts across phases, or cross-sectional organization level research that associates recruitment activities from multiple phases with organizational outcomes. The third approach is to recognize the distinctive nature of each phase and develop a solid understanding of each in its own right before attempting to study linkages between phases.

There is much to recommend the third approach. First, there are many unanswered questions at this level. Second, as Chapter 5 indicates, there are a number of technical difficulties associated with research that incorporates multiple phases. Third, beyond these technical difficulties, organization-level research often fails to provide *explanations* for effects. Therefore, one approach to building a comprehensive body of recruitment knowledge is to first develop a detailed understanding of what occurs *within* phases, ultimately using that knowledge to build well-grounded models of the overall recruitment process.

Guideline #3: Choose interesting and important questions

One hopes that researchers already know that it is good to address interesting and important questions. What is less clear, in the context of recruitment research, is exactly what makes a question interesting or important. I suggest that questions are more interesting and important to the extent that they (1) contribute to theories of human behavior, and (2) address applied problems.

A common complaint about existing recruitment research is that it is not sufficiently theoretical (Rynes, Heneman, & Schwab, 1980; Taylor & Giannantonio, 1993; Wanous & Collela, 1989). Recruitment research does lack an overarching theoretical model that would help focus and organize our research (Bacharach, 1989; Hall & Lindzey, 1978), and it seems unlikely that a single model capturing the essence of recruitment will emerge. Recruitment is a complex multistage process involving a variety of events, actors, and outcomes. It is hard to imagine a single explanation of recruitment that would be both comprehensive and parsimonious. In Whetten's (1989) terms, there are a large number of "whats" and "hows" to deal with. In addition, different rationale are required to explain the various aspects of recruitment (or, in Whetten's terms, there are a great many "whys").

However, recruitment is a fertile ground for the *application* of existing theories from the basic social sciences. The advantages of framing our questions in terms of such models are many. First, theories help us to understand *why* observed relationships exist. Second, they can help us understand circumstances under which our effects are more or less likely to be obtained. And third, studies that address recruitment issues through the application of basic theory make a dual contribution to the literature, enhancing our understanding of recruitment while at the same time providing additional evidence as to the validity of the theory.

Even as recruitment research is criticized for being insufficiently theoretical, human resource management research in general is being criticized for being insufficiently practical. Johns (1993), for instance, noted that techniques advocated by personnel researchers are adopted only infrequently by organizations. Campbell (1990) argued that we often fail to address questions that are critical to practitioners. Therefore, a second way to assess whether a research question is interesting or important is to consider its applied value. Too often, the recruitment questions raised by practitioners and the issues addressed by academics diverge (Rynes, 1991). Recruitment researchers should remain in close contact with both organizations and applicants to ensure that our studies have practical applications, as such relevance increases the value of our research.

Guideline #4: Be mindful of the need to accumulate research findings

One of the frustrations I experienced in writing this book was that relatively few recruitment topics have been the focus of sustained or systematic programs of research. Studies of recruitment source effects, realistic job previews, and reactions to initial interviews might be so categorized. But there are many other areas that are characterized by small numbers of loosely connected studies, each of which raises additional questions that too often go unaddressed. This fragmentation may be the reason that so few recruitment-related meta-analyses have been published: To date, the RJP literature has been examined meta-analytically by several authors (e.g., McEvoy & Cascio, 1985; Premack & Wanous, 1985), but to my knowledge this is the only area of recruitment for which such analyses are available.

Therefore, I recommend that recruitment researchers remain conscious of how their research fits into the existing literature. Does it build from what we already know? Does it provide additional insights? Will it help resolve questions that emerged in previous studies? It is unlikely that recruitment research will develop systematically if recruitment researchers are not systematic in their choice of research questions.

Concluding Remarks

Increasingly, the importance of human resources and of human resource policies as determinants of organizational effectiveness is being recognized by practitioners and by academics. In addition, though efforts to better accommodate nonwork interests are currently in the forefront of popular consciousness, it is very much the case that work will remain an essential part of most of our lives, and characteristics of the organization we choose to work for will have a significant influence on our quality of life. Therefore, recruitment has significant implications for both organizations and individuals.

As the preceding chapters document, there are many aspects of recruitment on which little research has been conducted. At present, the challenge for recruitment scholars lies not in identifying unanswered questions but in choosing wisely from the many questions that remain.

The guidelines offered above are meant to encourage conscious thought about what makes a particular recruitment research question appropriate as the "next step." They are not intended to be iron-clad rules, and there is certainly room for disagreement with my recommendations. My hope is that thoughtful consideration of the issues raised by these guidelines, in combination with the framework and reviews provided earlier in this volume, will lead to valuable advances in recruitment research.

References

Alderfer, C. P. (1969). An empirical test of a new theory of human needs. *Organizational Behavior and Human Performance, 4,* 142-175.

Alderfer, C. P., & McCord, C. G. (1970). Personal and situational factors in the recruitment interview. *Journal of Applied Psychology, 34,* 377-385.

Alvarez, P. H. (1991). Corporate advertising survey: Magazines, TV top '90 media lists. *Public Relations Journal, 47,* 14-15.

Arthur, J. B. (1994). Effects of human resource systems on manufacturing performance and turnover. *Academy of Management Journal, 37,* 670-687.

Arvey, R., Gordon, M., Massengill, D., & Mussio, S. (1975). Differential dropout rates of minority and majority job candidates due to time lags between selection procedures. *Personnel Psychology, 38,* 175-180.

Asch, B. J. (1990). Do incentives matter? The case of Navy recruiters. *Industrial and Labor Relations Review, 43,* 89S-106S.

Asch, S. E. (1946). Forming impressions of personality. *Journal of Abnormal and Social Psychology, 41,* 258-290.

Bacharach, S. B. (1989). Organizational theories: Some criteria for evaluation. *Academy of Management Review, 14,* 496-515.

Barber, A. E., & Daly, C. L. (1996). Compensation and diversity: New pay for a new workforce? In E. E. Kossek & S. A. Lobel (Eds.), *Managing diversity: Human resource strategies for transforming the workplace,* pp. 194-216. Cambridge, MA: Blackwell.

Barber, A. E., Daly, C. L., Giannantonio, C. M., & Phillips, J. M. (1994). Job search activities: An examination of changes over time. *Personnel Psychology, 47,* 739-766.

Barber, A. E., Dunham, R. L., & Formisano, R. A. (1992). The impact of flexible benefits on employee satisfaction: A field study. *Personnel Psychology, 45,* 55-75.

Barber, A. E., Hollenbeck, J. R., Tower, S. L., & Phillips, J. M. (1994). The effects of interview focus on recruitment effectiveness: A field experiment. *Journal of Applied Psychology, 79,* 886-896.

Barber, A. E., & Roehling, M. V. (1993). Job postings and the decision to interview: A verbal protocol analysis. *Journal of Applied Psychology, 78,* 845-856.

Bazerman, M. H., Schroth, H. A., Shah, P. P., Diekman, K. A., & Tenbrunsel, A. E. (1994). The inconsistent role of comparison others and procedural justice in reactions to hypothetical job descriptions: Implications for job acceptance decisions. *Organizational Behavior and Human Decision Processes, 60,* 326-352.

Becker, B., & Gerhart, B. (1996). The impact of human resource management on organizational performance: Progress and prospects. *Academy of Management Journal, 39,* 779-801.

Behling, O., Labovitz, G., & Gainer, M. (1968). College recruiting: A theoretical basis. *Personnel Journal, 47,* 13-19.

Belt, J. A., & Paolillo, J. G. P. (1982). The influence of corporate image and specificity of candidate qualifications on response to recruitment advertisement. *Journal of Management, 8,* 105-112.

Billings, R. S., & Scherer, L. L. (1988). The effects of response mode and importance on decision-making strategies: Judgment versus choice. *Organizational Behavior and Human Decision Processes, 41,* 1-19.

Blau, G. (1990). Exploring the mediating mechanisms affecting the relationship of recruitment source to employee performance. *Journal of Vocational Behavior, 37,* 303-320.

Blau, D. M. (1992). An empirical analysis of employed and unemployed job search behavior. *Industrial and Labor Relations Review, 45,* 738-752.

Boudreau, J. W. (1991). Utility analysis for decisions in human resource management. In M. D. Dunnette & L. M. Hough (Eds.), *Handbook of Industrial and Organizational Psychology* (2nd ed., Vol. 2, pp. 621-746). Palo Alto, CA: Consulting Psychologists Press.

Boudreau, J. W., & Rynes, S. L. (1985). Role of recruitment in staffing utility analysis. *Journal of Applied Psychology, 70,* 354-366.

Breaugh, J. A. (1992). *Recruitment: Science and practice.* Boston: PWS-Kent Publishing.

Breaugh, J. A. (1983). Realistic job previews: A critical appraisal and future research directions. *Academy of Management Review, 8,* 612-619.

Breaugh, J. A. (1981). Relationships between recruiting sources and employee performance, absenteeism, and work attitudes. *Academy of Management Journal, 24,* 142-147.

Breaugh, J. A., & Mann, R. B. (1984). Recruiting source effects: A test of two alternative explanations. *Journal of Occupational Psychology, 57,* 261-267.

Brett, J. M., Stroh, L. K., & Reilly, A. H. (1992). Job transfer. In C. L. Cooper & I. T. Robertson (Eds.), *International Review of Industrial and Organizational Psychology.* Chicester, England: Wiley.

Bretz, R. D., Jr., Ash, R. A., & Dreher, G. F. (1989). Do people make the place? An examination of the attraction-selection-attrition hypothesis. *Personnel Psychology, 42,* 561-581.

Bretz, R. D., Jr., & Judge, T. A. (1994). The role of human resource systems in job applicant decision processes. *Journal of Management, 20,* 531-551.

Brown, K. A., & Huber, V. L. (1992). Lowering floors and raising ceilings: A longitudinal assessment of the effects of an earnings-at-risk plan on pay satisfaction. *Personnel Psychology, 45,* 279-312.

Bureau of National Affairs. (1988). Recruiting and selection procedures. *Personnel Policies Forum, 146.* Washington, DC: Bureau of National Affairs, Inc.

Cable, D. M., & Judge, T. A. (1994). Pay preferences and job search decisions: A person-organization fit perspective. *Personnel Psychology, 47,* 317-348.

Cable, D. M., & Judge, T. A. (1996). Person-organization fit, job choice decisions, and organizational entry. *Organizational Behavior and Human Decision Processes, 67,* 294-311.

Caldwell, D. F., & Spivey, W. A. (1983). The relationship between recruiting source and employee success: An analysis by race. *Personnel Psychology, 36,* 67-72.

Campbell, J. P. (1990). The role of theory in industrial and organizational psychology. In M. D. Dunnette & L. M. Hough (Eds.), *Handbook of Industrial and Organizational Psychology* (2nd ed., Vol. 1, pp. 39-74). Palo Alto, CA: Consulting Psychologists Press.

Carruthers, W. E., & Pinder, C. C. (1983). Urban geographic factors and location satisfaction following a personnel transfer. *Academy of Management Journal, 26,* 520-526.

Cascio, W. F., & Phillips, N. F. (1979). Performance testing: A rose among thorns? *Personnel Psychology, 32,* 751-766.

Chan, D. (1997). Racial subgroup differences in predictive validity perceptions on personality and cognitive ability tests. *Journal of Applied Psychology, 82,* 311-320.

Chan, D., & Schmitt, N. (1997). Video-based versus paper-and-pencil method of assessment in situational judgment tests: Subgroup differences in test performance and face validity perceptions. *Journal of Applied Psychology, 82,* 143-159.

Chan, D., Schmitt, N., DeShon, R. P., Clause, C. S., & Delbridge, K. (1997). Reactions to cognitive ability tests: The relationships between race, test performance, face validity perceptions, and test-taking motivation. *Journal of Applied Psychology, 82,* 300-310.

Chatman, J. A. (1989). Improving interactional organizational research: A model of person-organization fit. *Academy of Management Review, 14,* 333-349.

Chatman, J. A. (1991). Matching people and organizations: Selection and socialization in public accounting firms. *Administrative Science Quarterly, 36,* 459-484.

Christie, J., & Klein, R. (1995). Familiarity and attention: Does what we know affect what we notice? *Memory and Cognition, 23,* 547-550.

Colarelli, S. M. (1984). Methods of communication and mediating processes in realistic job previews. *Journal of Applied Psychology, 69,* 633-642.

Cooper, W. H., & Richardson, A. J. (1986). Unfair comparisons. *Journal of Applied Psychology, 71,* 179-184.

Crant, J. M., & Bateman, T. S. (1990). An experimental test of the impact of drug-testing programs on potential job applicants' attitudes and intentions. *Journal of Applied Psychology, 75,* 127-131.

Dawis, R. V., Lofquist, L. H., & Weiss, D. J. (1968). A theory of work adjustment. *Minnesota Studies in Vocational Rehabilitation, 23* (IRC Bulletin No. 47).

Decker, P. J., & Cornelius, E. T. III. (1979). A note on recruiting sources and job satisfaction. *Journal of Applied Psychology, 64,* 463-464.

Delaney, J. T., & Huselid, M. A. (1996). The impact of human resource management practices on perceptions of organizational performance. *Academy of Management Journal, 39,* 949-969.

Dichter, E. (1985). What's in an image. *Journal of Consumer Marketing, 2,* 109-115.

Dutton, J. E., Dukerich, J. M., & Harquail, C. V. (1994). Organizational images and member identification. *Administrative Science Quarterly, 39,* 239-263.

Eden, D., & Aviram, A. (1993). Self-efficacy training to speed reemployment: Helping people to help themselves. *Journal of Applied Psychology, 78,* 352-360.

Einhorn, H. J., Kleinmuntz, D. N., & Kleinmuntz, B. (1979). Linear regression and process-tracing models of judgment. *Psychological Review, 86,* 465-485.

Eisenhart, K. (1989). Agency theory: An assessment and review. *Academy of Management Review, 1,* 57-74.

Ellis, R. A., & Taylor, M. S. (1983). Role of self-esteem within the job search process. *Journal of Applied Psychology, 68,* 632-640.

Feldman, D. C., & Arnold, H. J. (1978). Position choice: Comparing the importance of organizational and job factors. *Journal of Applied Psychology, 63,* 706-710.

Festinger, L. (1957). *A Theory of Cognitive Dissonance.* Evanston, IL: Row, Peterson.

Fisher, A. (1997, October 27). The world's most admired companies. *Fortune, 136*(8), 220-240.

Fombrun, C., & Shanley, M. (1990). What's in a name? Reputation building and corporate strategy. *Academy of Management Journal, 33,* 233-258.

Gannon, M. J. (1971). Sources of referral and employee turnover. *Journal of Applied Psychology, 55,* 226-228.

Gatewood, R. D., Gowan, M. A., & Lautenschlager, G. J. (1993). Corporate image, recruitment image, and initial job choice decisions. *Academy of Management Journal, 36,* 414-427.

Gellerman, S. (1964). *Motivation and Productivity.* New York: American Management Association.

Gilliland, S. W. (1994). Effects of procedural and distributive justice on reactions to a selection system. *Journal of Applied Psychology, 79,* 691-701.

Gilliland, S. W. (1993). The perceived fairness of selection systems: An organizational justice perspective. *Academy of Management Review, 18,* 694-734.

Glickstein, G., & Ramer, D. C. Z. (1988, February). The alternative employment marketplace. *Personnel Administrator,* 100-104.

Glueck, W. F. (1974). Decision making: Organizational choice. *Personnel Psychology, 27,* 77-93.

Golden, L. L., Albaum, G., & Zimmer, M. (1987). The numerical comparative score: An economical format for retail image measurement. *Journal of Retailing, 63,* 393-410.

Goltz, S. M., & Giannantonio, C. M. (1995). Recruiter friendliness and attraction to the job: The mediating role of inferences about the organization. *Journal of Vocational Behavior, 46,* 109-118.

Graves, L. M. (1993). Sources of individual differences in interviewer effectiveness: A model and implications for future research. *Journal of Organizational Behavior, 14,* 349-370.

Griffeth, R. W., Hom, P. W., Fink, L. S., & Cohen, D. J. (1997). Comparative tests of multivariate models of recruiting sources effects. *Journal of Management, 23,* 19-36.

Guion, R. M. (1976). Recruiting, selection, and job placement. In M. D. Dunnette (Ed.), *Handbook of Industrial and Organizational Psychology,* pp. 777-828. Chicago: Rand-McNally.

Hall, C. S., & Lindzey, G. (1978). *Theories of Personality* (3rd ed.). New York: Wiley.

Harris, M. M., & Fink, L. S. (1987). A field study of applicant reactions to employment opportunities: Does the recruiter make a difference? *Personnel Psychology, 40,* 765-783.

Heneman, H. G. III, & Heneman, R.L. (1994). *Staffing Organizations.* Madison, WI: Mendota House.

Herriot, P. (1993). A paradigm bursting at the seams. *Journal of Organizational Behavior, 14,* 371-375.

Herriot, P. (1989). Selection as a social process. In M. Smith & I. T. Robertson (Eds.), *Advances in Selection and Assessment,* pp. 171-187, Chichester, England: Wiley.

Herriot, P., & Rothwell, C. (1981). Organizational choice and decision theory: Effects of employers' literature and selection interview. *Journal of Occupational Psychology, 54,* 17-31.

Hogarth, R. M., & Einhorn, H. J. (1976). Optimal strategies for personnel selection when candidates can reject offers. *The Journal of Business, 49,* 478-495.

Honeycutt, T. L., & Rosen, B. (1997). *Journal of Vocational Behavior, 50,* 271-290.

Huber, V. L., Northcraft, G. B., & Neale, M. A. (1990). Effects of decision strategy and number of openings on employment selection decisions. *Organizational Behavior and Human Decision Processes, 45,* 276-284.

Huselid, M. A. (1995). The impact of human resource management practices on turnover, productivity, and corporate financial performance. *Academy of Management Journal, 38,* 635-672.

Irving, G. P., & Meyer, J. P. (1994). Reexamination of the met-expectations hypothesis: A longitudinal analysis. *Journal of Applied Psychology, 79,* 937-949.

Jackson, S. E., Brett, J. F., Sessa, V. I., Cooper, D. M., Julin, J. A., & Peyronnin, K. (1991). Some differences make a difference: Individual dissimilarity and group heterogeneity as correlates of recruitment, promotions, and turnover. *Journal of Applied Psychology, 76,* 675-689.

Johns, G. (1993). Constraints on the adoption of psychology-based personnel practices: Lessons from organizational innovation. *Personnel Psychology, 46,* 569-592.

Judge, T. A., & Bretz, R. D., Jr. (1992). Effects of work values on job choice decisions. *Journal of Applied Psychology, 77,* 261-271.

Judge, T. A., & Cable, D. M. (1997). Applicant personality, organizational culture, and organization attraction. *Personnel Psychology, 50,* 359-394.

Jurgensen, C. E. (1978). Job preferences (What makes a job good or bad?). *Journal of Applied Psychology, 63,* 267-276.

Katayama, H. (1990, October 15) Lightening up heavy. *Forbes,* 42-43.

Kelley, B. (1993, March). So who did they hire? *Across the Board, 30,*(2), 28-32.

Kirnan, J. P., Farley, J. A., & Geisinger, K. F. (1989). The relationship between recruiting source, applicant quality, and hire performance: An analysis by sex, ethnicity, and age. *Personnel Psychology, 42,* 293-308.

Koch, J. (1990, February). Beyond nuts and bolts. *Personnel Journal, 69,*70-77.

Koch, J. (1989, October). Ads with flair. *Personnel Journal, 68,* 46-55.

Kristof, A. L. (1996). Person-organization fit: An integrative review of its conceptualizations, measurement, and implications. *Personnel Psychology, 49,* 1-50.

Kumar, N., Stern, L. W., & Anderson, J. C. (1993). Conducting interorganizational research using key informants. *Academy of Management Journal, 36,* 1614-1632.

Laabs, J. J. (1991). Nurses get critical about recruitment ads. *Personnel Journal, 70,*(7), 63-69.

Lacy, W. B., Bokemeier, J. L., & Shepard, J. M. (1983). Job attribute preferences and work commitment of men and women in the United States. *Personnel Psychology, 36,* 315-329.

Landy, F. J., Farr, J. L., & Jacobs, R. R. (1982). Utility concepts in performance measurement. *Organizational Behavior and Human Performance, 30,* 15-40.

Latham, G. P., & Whyte, G. (1994). The futility of utility analysis. *Personnel Psychology, 47,* 31-46.

Law, K. S., & Myors, B. (1993). Cutoff scores that maximize the total utility of a selection program: Comment on Martin and Raju's (1992) procedure. *Journal of Applied Psychology, 78,* 736-740.

Lawler, E. E., Kuleck, W. J., Rhode, J. G., & Sorensen, J. E. (1975). Job choice and post decision dissonance. *Organizational Behavior and Human Performance, 13,* 133-145.

Lefkowitz, J. (1994). Sex-related differences in job attitudes and dispositional variables: Now you see them . . . *Academy of Management Journal, 37,* 323-349.

Leister, D. V., & Machlachlan, D. L. (1975). Organizational self-perception and environmental image measurement. *Academy of Management Journal, 18,* 205-223.

Liden, R. C., & Parsons, C. K. (1986). A field study of job applicant interview perceptions, alternative opportunities, and demographic characteristics. *Personnel Psychology, 39,* 109-123.

Lippman, S., & McCall, J. (1976). The economics of job search: A survey. Part 1. *Economic Inquiry, 14,* 155-190.

Macan, T. H., Avedon, M. J., Paese, M., & Smith, D. E. (1994). The effects of applicants' reactions to cognitive ability tests and an assessment center. *Personnel Psychology, 47,* 715-738.

Macan, T. H., & Dipboye, R. L. (1990). The relationship of interviewers' preinterview impressions to selection and recruitment outcomes. *Personnel Psychology, 43,* 745-768.

MacDuffie, J. P. (1995). Human resource bundles and manufacturing performance: Organizational logic and flexible production systems in the world auto industry. *Industrial and Labor Relations Review, 48,* 197-221.

Mamarchev, S. (1996, October). Think like a marketing pro. *HR Focus, 73,*(10), 9-10.

Martin, B. (1987, August). Recruitment Adventures. *Personnel Journal, 66,* 46-63.

Martin, S. L., & Raju, N. S. (1992). Determining cutoff scores that optimize utility: A recognition of recruiting costs. *Journal of Applied Psychology, 77,* 15-23.

Mason, N. A., & Belt, J. A. (1986). Effectiveness of specificity in recruitment advertising. *Journal of Management, 12,* 425-432.

Maurer, S. D., Howe, V., & Lee, T. W. (1992). Organizational recruiting as marketing management: An interdisciplinary study of engineering graduates. *Personnel Psychology, 45,* 807-833.

McCarthy, A. H. (1989, August). Recruitment: Research provides advertising focus. *Personnel Journal, 68,* 82-86.

McEvoy, G. M., & Cascio, W. F. (1985). Strategies for reducing employee turnover: A meta-analysis. *Journal of Applied Psychology, 70,* 342-353.

Meglino, B. M., DeNisi, A. S., & Ravlin, E. C. (1993). Effects of previous job exposure and subsequent job status on the functioning of a realistic job preview. *Personnel Psychology, 46,* 803-822.

Meglino, B. M., DeNisi, A. S., Youngblood, S. A., & Williams, K. J. (1988). Effects of realistic job previews: A comparison using an enhancement and a reduction preview. *Journal of Applied Psychology, 73,* 259-266.

Mellers, B. A., Richards, V., & Birnbaum, M. H. (1992). Distributional theories of impression formation. *Organizational Behavior and Human Decision Processes, 51,* 313-343.

Minnehan, M. (1997, March). What the future holds for HR. *HRMagazine, 42,*(3), 116-118.

Mitchell, T. R., & Beach, L. R. (1976). A review of occupational preference and choice research using expectancy theory and decision theory. *Journal of Occupational Psychology, 49,* 231-248.

Morita, J. G., Lee, T. W., & Mowday, R. T. (1989). Introducing survival analysis to organizational researchers: A selected application to turnover research. *Journal of Applied Psychology, 74,* 280-292.

Murphy, K. R. (1986). When your top choice turns you down: Effect of rejected offers on the utility of selection tests. *Psychological Bulletin, 99,* 133-138.

Nakache, P. (1997, September 29). Cisco's recruiting edge. *Fortune, 136*(6), 275-276.

Noe, R. A., & Barber, A. E. (1993). Willingness to accept mobility opportunities: Destination makes a difference. *Journal of Organizational Behavior, 14,* 159-175.

Noe, R. A., Steffy, B. D., & Barber, A. E. (1988). An investigation of the factors influencing employees' willingness to accept mobility opportunities. *Personnel Psychology, 41,* 559-580.

O'Keefe, B. J., & Delia, J. G. (1982). Impression formation and message production. In M. E. Roloff & C. R. Berger (Eds.), *Social Cognition and Communication,* 33-72. Beverly Hills, CA: Sage.

O'Reilly, C. A. III, & Caldwell, D. F. (1980). Job choice: The impact of intrinsic and extrinsic factors on subsequent satisfaction and commitment. *Journal of Applied Psychology, 65,* 559-565.

O'Reilly, C. A., Chatman, J. A., & Caldwell, D. F. (1991). People and organizational culture: A profile comparison approach to assessing person-organization fit. *Academy of Management Journal, 34,* 487-516.

Osborn, D. P. (1990). A reexamination of the organizational choice process. *Journal of Vocational Behavior, 36,* 45-60.

Pfeffer, J. (1994). *Competitive Advantage through People.* Boston: Harvard Business School Press.

Pinder, C. C. (1989). The dark side of executive relocation. *Organizational Dynamics, 17,* 48-58.

Pinder, C. C. (1977). Multiple predictors of post-transfer satisfaction: The role of urban factors. *Personnel Psychology, 30,* 543-566.

Pinder, C. C., & Schroeder, K. G. (1987). Time to proficiency following job transfers. *Academy of Management Journal, 30,* 336-353.

Powell, G. N. (1984). Effects of job attributes and recruiting practices on applicant decisions: A comparison. *Personnel Psychology, 37,* 721-732.

Powell, G. N. (1991). Applicant reactions to the initial employment interview: Exploring theoretical and methodological issues. *Personnel Psychology, 44,* 67-83.

Powell, G. N., & Goulet, L. R. (1996). Recruiters' and applicants' reactions to campus interviews and employment decisions. *Academy of Management Journal, 39,* 1619-1640.

Power, D. J., & Aldag, R. J. (1985). Soelberg's job search and choice model: A clarification, review, and critique. *Academy of Management Review, 10,* 48-58.

Premack, S. L., & Wanous, J. P. (1985). A meta-analysis of realistic job preview experiments. *Journal of Applied Psychology, 70,* 706-719.

Quaglieri, P. L. (1982). A note on variations in recruiting information obtained through different sources. *Journal of Occupational Psychology, 55,* 53-55.

Redman, T., & Mathews, B. P. (1992). Advertising for effective managerial recruitment. *Journal of General Management, 18,* 29-44.

Reilly, R. R., Brown, B., Blood, M. R., & Malatesta, C. Z. (1981). The effects of realistic previews: A study and discussion of the literature. *Personnel Psychology, 34,* 823-834.

Reynolds, L. G. (1951). *The Structure of Labor Markets.* New York: Harper.

Rosse, J. G., Miller, J. L., & Stecher, M. D. (1994). A field study of applicants' reactions to personality and cognitive ability testing. *Journal of Applied Psychology, 79,* 987-992.

Rottenberg, S. (1956). On choice in labor markets. *Industrial and Labor Relations Review, 9,* 183-199.

Rynes, S. L. (1991). Recruitment, job choice, and post-hire consequences. In M. D. Dunnette & L. M. Hough (Eds.), *Handbook of Industrial and Organizational Psychology* (2nd ed.). Palo Alto, CA: Consulting Psychologists Press.

Rynes, S. L. (1989). The employment interview as a recruitment device. In R. W. Eder & G. R. Ferris (Eds.), *The Employment Interview: Theory, Research, and Practice,* pp. 127-142. Newbury Park, CA: Sage.

Rynes, S. L. (1986). Compensation strategies for recruiting. *Topics in Total Compensation, 2,* 185-196.

Rynes, S. L., & Barber, A. E. (1990). Applicant attraction strategies: An organizational perspective. *Academy of Management Review, 15,* 286-310.

Rynes, S. L., & Boudreau, J. W. (1986). College recruiting in large organizations: Practice, evaluation, and research implications. *Personnel Psychology, 39,* 729-757.

Rynes, S. L., Bretz, R. D., Jr., & Gerhart, B. (1991). The importance of recruitment in job choice: A different way of looking. *Personnel Psychology, 44,* 487-521.

Rynes, S. L., & Connerly, M. L. (1993). Applicant reactions to alternative selection procedures. *Journal of Business and Psychology, 7,* 261-277.

Rynes, S. L., & Gerhart, B. (1990). Interviewer assessments of applicant "fit": An exploratory investigation. *Personnel Psychology, 43,* 13-35.

Rynes, S. L., Heneman, H. G. III, & Schwab, D. P. (1980). Individual reactions to organizational recruiting: A review. *Personnel Psychology, 33,* 529-542.

Rynes, S. L., & Lawler, J. (1983). A policy-capturing investigation of the role of expectancies in decisions to pursue job alternative. *Journal of Applied Psychology, 68,* 620-631.

Rynes, S. L., & Miller, H. E. (1983). Recruiter and job influences on candidates for employment. *Journal of Applied Psychology, 68,* 146-154.

Rynes, S. L., Orlitzky, M. O., & Bretz, R. D. (1997). Experienced hiring vs. college recruiting: Practices and emerging trends. *Personnel Psychology, 50,* 309-340.

Rynes, S. L., Schwab, D. P., & Heneman, H. G. (1983). The role of pay and market pay variability in job application decisions. *Organizational Behavior and Human Performance, 31,* 353-364.

Saks, A. M., & Cronshaw, S. F. (1990). A process investigation of realistic job previews: Mediating variables and channels of communication. *Journal of Organizational Behavior, 11,* 221-236.

Saks, A. M., Leck, J. D., & Saunders, D. M. (1995). Effects of application blanks and employment equity on applicant reactions and job pursuit intentions. *Journal of Organizational Behavior, 16,* 415-430.

Saks, A. M., Wiesner, W. H., & Summers, R. J. (1994). Effects of job previews on self-selection and job choice. *Journal of Vocational Behavior, 44,* 297-316.

Saks, A. M., Wiesner, W. H., & Summers, R. J. (1996). Effects of job previews and compensation policy on applicant attraction and job choice. *Journal of Vocational Behavior, 49,* 68-85.

Schmidt, F. L., Greenthal, A. L., Hunter, J. E., Berner, J. G., & Seaton, F. W. (1977). Job sample vs. paper-and-pencil trades and technical tests: Adverse impact and examinee attitudes. *Personnel Psychology, 30,* 187-197.

Schmitt, N., & Coyle, B. W. (1976). Applicant decisions in the employment interview. *Journal of Applied Psychology, 61,* 184-192.

Schmitt, N., & Schneider, B. (1983). Current issues in personnel selection. In K. R. Rowland and G. Ferris (Eds.), *Research in Personnel and Human Resources Management* (Vol. 1, pp. 85-125). Greenwich, CT: JAI Press.

Schneider, B. (1987). The people make the place. *Personnel Psychology, 40,* 437-453.

RT = Schwab, D. P. (1982). Recruiting and organizational participation. In K. Rowland & G. Ferris (Eds.), *Personnel Management,* 103-128. Boston: Allyn & Bacon.

Schwab, D. P., Rynes, S. L., & Aldag, R. A. (1987). Theories and research on job search and choice. In K. Rowland and G. Ferris (Eds.), *Research in Personnel and Human Resource Management* (Vol. 5, pp. 129-166). Greenwich, CT: JAI Press.

Schwoerer, C., & Rosen, B. (1989). Effects of employment at will policies and compensation policies on corporate image and job pursuit intentions. *Journal of Applied Psychology, 74,* 653-656.

Sheridan, J. E., Richards, M. D., & Slocum, J. W. (1975). Comparative analysis of expectancy and heuristic models of decision behavior. *Journal of Applied Psychology, 60,* 361-368.

Simon, H. A. (1947). *Administrative behavior.* New York: Macmillan.

Smither, J. W., Reilly, R. R., Millsap, R. E., Pearlman, K., & Stoffey, R. W. (1993). Applicant reactions to selection procedures. *Personnel Psychology, 46,* 49-76.

Soelberg, P. O. (1967). Unprogrammed decision making. *Industrial Management Review, 8,* 19-29.

Spence, A. M. (1974). *Market Signalling.* Cambridge, MA: Harvard University Press.

Spence, A. M. (1973). Job market signalling. *Quarterly Journal of Economics, 87,* 355-374.

Steiner, D., & Gilliland, S. W. (1996). Fairness reactions to personnel selection techniques in France and the United States. *Journal of Applied Psychology, 81,* 134-141.

Stevens, C. K. (1997). Effects of preinterview beliefs on applicants' reactions to campus interviews. *Academy of Management Journal, 40,* 947-966.

Stevens, C. K., Mitchell, T. R., & Tripp, T. (1990). Order of presentation and verbal recruitment strategy effectiveness. *Journal of Applied Social Psychology, 20,* 1076-1092.

Stevens, C. K. (In press). Antecedents of interview interactions, interviewers' ratings, and applicants' reactions. *Personnel Psychology, 51.*

Stewart, T. A. (1996). Taking on the last bureaucracy. *Fortune, 133*(1), 105-108. New York: Time Inc.

Stigler, G. (1962). Information in the labor market. *Journal of Political Economy, 70,* 49-73.

Stone, E. F., & Stone, D. L. (1990). Privacy in organizations: Theoretical issues, research findings, and protection mechanisms. In K. R. Rowland & G. Ferris (Eds.), *Research in Personnel and Human Resource Management* (Vol. 8, pp. 349-411). Greenwich, CT: JAI Press.

Suszko, M. J., & Breaugh, J. A. (1986). The effects of realistic job previews on applicant self-selection and employee turnover, satisfaction, and coping ability. *Journal of Management, 12,* 513-523.

Sutton, R. I., & Staw, B. M. (1995). What theory is not. *Administrative Science Quarterly, 40,* 371-384.

Tajfel, H., & Turner, J. C. (1985). The social identity theory of group behavior. In S. Worchel & W. G. Austin (Eds.), *Psychology of Intergroup Relations* (Vol. 2, pp. 7-24). Chicago: Nelson-Hall.

Taylor, M. S., & Bergmann, T. J. (1987). Organizational recruitment activities and applicants' reactions at different stages of the recruitment process. *Personnel Psychology, 40,* 261-285.

Taylor, M. S., & Giannantonio, C. M. (1993). Forming, adapting, and terminating the employment relationship: A review of the literature from individual, organizational, and interactionist perspectives. *Journal of Management, 19,* 461-515.

Taylor, M. S., & Schmidt, D. W. (1983). A process-oriented investigation of recruitment source effectiveness. *Personnel Psychology,* 343-354.

Taylor, M. S., & Sniezek, J. A. (1984). The college recruitment interview: Topical content and applicant reactions. *Journal of Occupational Psychology, 57,* 157-168.

Terpstra, D. E. (1996). The search for effective methods. *HR Focus, 73*(5), 16-17.

Terpstra, D. E., & Rozell, E. J. (1993). The relationship of staffing practices to organizational level measures of performance. *Personnel Psychology, 46,* 27-48.

Tom, V. R. (1971). The role of personality and organizational images in the recruiting process. *Organizational Behavior and Human Performance, 6,* 573-592.

Tullar, W. L. (1989). Relational control in the employment interview. *Journal of Applied Psychology, 74,* 971-977.

Tully, S. (1996, September 30). Wall Street pay: These raises are insane! *Fortune, 134*(6), 168-170.

Turban, D. B., Campion, J. E., & Eyring, A. R. (1995). Factors related to job acceptance decisions of college recruits. *Journal of Vocational Behavior, 47,* 193-213.

Turban, D. B., & Dougherty, T. W. (1992). Influences of campus recruiting on applicant attraction to firms. *Academy of Management Journal, 35,* 739-765.

Turban, D. B., Eyring, A. R., & Campion, J. E. (1993). Job attributes: Preferences compared with reasons given for accepting and rejecting job offers. *Journal of Occupational and Organizational Psychology, 66,* 71-81.

Turban, D. B., & Greening, D. W. (1997). Corporate social performance and organizational attractiveness to prospective employees. *Academy of Management Journal, 40,* 658-672.

Tversky, A. (1972). Choice by elimination. *Journal of Mathematical Psychology, 9,* 341-367.

Tversky, A., & Kahneman, D. (1974). Judgment under uncertainty: Heuristics and biases. *Science, 185,* 1124-1131.

Ulrich, D. (1997). *Human resource champions: The next agenda for adding value and delivering results.* Boston: Harvard Business School Press.

Vecchio, R. P. (1995). The impact of referral sources on employee attitudes: Evidence from a national sample. *Journal of Management, 21,* 953-965.

Vinokur, A. D., van Ryn, M., Gramlich, E. M., & Price, R. H. (1991). Long-term follow-up and benefit-cost analysis of the jobs program: A preventive intervention for the unemployed. *Journal of Applied Psychology, 76,* 213-219.

Vroom, V. H. (1964). *Work and motivation.* New York: Wiley.

Vroom, V. H. (1966). Organizational choice: A study of pre- and postdecision processes. *Organizational Behavior and Human Performance, 1,* 212-225.

Wanous, J. P. (1992). *Organizational entry: Recruitment, selection, orientation and Socialization of newcomers* (2nd ed.). Reading, MA: Addison-Wesley.

Wanous, J. P. (1980). *Organizational entry: Recruitment, selection, orientation and socialization of newcomers.* Reading, MA: Addison-Wesley.

Wanous, J. P. (1978). Realistic job previews: Can a procedure to reduce turnover also influence the relationship between abilities and performance? *Personnel Psychology, 31,* 249-258.

Wanous, J. P. (1977). Organizational entry: Newcomers moving from outside to inside. *Psychological Bulletin, 84,* 601-618.

Wanous, J. P. (1973). Effects of a realistic job preview on job acceptance, job attitudes, and job survival. *Journal of Applied Psychology, 58,* 327-332.

Wanous, J. P., & Colella, A. (1989). Organizational entry research: Current status and future directions. In K. Rowland & G. Ferris (Eds.), *Research In Personnel and Human Resources Management* (Volume 7, pp. 59-120). Greenwich, CT: JAI Press.

Wanous, J. P., Keon, T. L., & Latack, J. C. (1983). Expectancy theory and occupational/organizational choice: A review and test. *Organizational Behavior and Human Performance, 32,* 66-86.

Weick, K. E. (1989). Theory construction as disciplined imagination. *Academy of Management Review, 14,* 516-531.

Weick, K. E. (1995). What theory is not, theorizing is. *Administrative Science Quarterly, 40,* 385-390.

Weisner, W. H., Saks, A. M., & Summers, R. J. (1991). Job alternatives and job choice. *Journal of Vocational Behavior, 38,* 198-207.

Welbourne, T. M., & Andrews, A. O. (1996). Predicting the performance of initial public offerings: Should human resource management be in the equation? *Academy of Management Journal, 39*, 891-919.

Werbel, J. D., & Landau, J. (1996). The effectiveness of different recruitment sources: A mediating variable analysis. *Journal of Applied Social Psychology, 26*, 1337-1350.

Whetten, D. A. (1989). What constitutes a theoretical contribution? *Academy of Management Review, 14*, 490-495.

Wiersma, U. J. (1990). Gender differences in job attribute preferences: Work-home role conflict and job level as mediating variables. *Journal of Occupational Psychology, 63*, 231-243.

Williams, M. L., & Bauer, T. N. (1994). The effect of a managing diversity policy on organizational attractiveness. *Group & Organization Management, 19*, 295-308.

Williams, M. L., & Dreher, G. F. (1992). Compensation system attributes and applicant pool characteristics. *Academy of Management Journal, 35*, 571-595.

Williams, C. R., Labig, C. E., & Stone, T. H. (1993). Recruitment sources and posthire outcomes for job applicants and new hires: A test of two hypotheses. *Journal of Applied Psychology, 78*, 163-172.

Yeager, P. L. (1991, September). The right image for recruitment. *The National Public Accountant*, 18-19.

Zedeck, S. (1977). An information processing model and approach to the study of motivation. *Organizational Behavior and Human Performance, 18*, 47-77.

Index

About the Author

Alison E. Barber (Ph.D., University of Wisconsin) is Associate Professor of Management at the Eli Broad Graduate School of Management at Michigan State University. She has been on the Michigan State faculty since graduating from the Industrial Relations Research Institute of the University of Wisconsin-Madison. She has published research articles on a number of topics associated with recruitment and job search, in such journals as *Journal of Applied Psychology, Personnel Psychology,* and *Academy of Management Review.*

Professor Barber also has significant practical experience in recruitment and human resource management. Prior to obtaining her doctorate, she was employed by General Mills and Chevron and was involved in recruitment activities at both organizations.

Printed in the United Kingdom
by Lightning Source UK Ltd.
124998UK00002B/127/A